# A Journey Towards Health

## REVERSING SCLERODERMA

Jane M. Parker
and
Victor Dyment

Writing assistance: Elieba Levine

Author's Note
This is a true story.
Some of the names have been changed
to protect private individuals.

Note for Librarians: A cataloguing record for this book is available from Library and Archives Canada at www.collectionscanada.ca/amicus/index-e.html
ISBN 1-4120-6291-8

*Printed in Victoria, BC, Canada. Printed on paper with minimum 30% recycled fibre. Trafford's print shop runs on "green energy" from solar, wind and other environmentally-friendly power sources.*

TRAFFORD PUBLISHING™

*Offices in Canada, USA, Ireland and UK*
This book was published *on-demand* in cooperation with Trafford Publishing. On-demand publishing is a unique process and service of making a book available for retail sale to the public taking advantage of on-demand manufacturing and Internet marketing. On-demand publishing includes promotions, retail sales, manufacturing, order fulfilment, accounting and collecting royalties on behalf of the author.

**Book sales for North America and international:**
Trafford Publishing, 6E–2333 Government St.,
Victoria, BC V8T 4P4 CANADA
phone 250 383 6864 (toll-free 1 888 232 4444)
fax 250 383 6804; email to orders@trafford.com
**Book sales in Europe:**
Trafford Publishing (UK) Ltd., Enterprise House, Wistaston Road Business Centre,
Wistaston Road, Crewe, Cheshire CW2 7RP UNITED KINGDOM
phone 01270 251 396 (local rate 0845 230 9601)
facsimile 01270 254 983; orders.uk@trafford.com
**Order online at:**
trafford.com/05-1192

10 9 8 7 6 5 4 3 2 1

# A Journey Towards Health

For our children
And the future generations
To provide necessary knowledge
for leading a healthy life

# Contents

# Introduction

WHEN MY DOCTOR FIRST GAVE me the diagnosis of a disease I had never heard of, it was surprising. With no previous knowledge of what Scleroderma could do to your body, I wasn't overly concerned. Always having been healthy and seemingly in control of every situation led me to believe there should be no problem in overcoming anything thrown at me. When I finally received a correct diagnosis, there seemed to be no reason to think it would not be treatable. I didn't realize how wrong I could be. Research on the disease showed me how badly Scleroderma could affect the body. I couldn't believe that this sort of deterioration and pain would happen, especially to me. The reports indicated that I might actually die from this disease. There was no available treatment that could cure it. The fact that I had an incurable and ultimately fatal disease was unacceptable. My only hope was to be optimistic. The belief that I would find the answers and reverse my increasingly declining health became my only reality. There would be no giving up. I didn't want to die. That was not in the picture. I was determined to return to full health, even though no one else had found any effective treatment for Scleroderma.

Instead of the diagnosis giving me answers, it just raised a whole new set of questions. According to all the Doctor's reports, there was no cure. This meant that some piece of information was missing. Being the type of person who always finds a way to get the necessary results and solutions, it was not even in my realm of possibility that this disease wouldn't be turned around. My goal was to become completely healthy again.

I didn't care if it was Scleroderma or any other fatal disease, there was no way that an illness would get the better of me. My friends were supportive of my declarations of returning to health. They knew about my personality, nothing could stop me once my mind was made up. They probably thought I was a little crazy being so optimistic, but they were kind and helped in my search for answers. Realizing it was up to me to find a way to cure myself, I began by looking on the Internet to see what other people had done. It surprised me to find that there were no treatment suggestions for Scleroderma. Nothing was written about how to heal the symptoms that arose. There was nothing said about how to cure this disease. The majority of advice was on how to cope. Even then, it was for a limited lifestyle and shortened amount of time. I didn't want to cope. I wanted to live a healthy life. I didn't want to become one of the statistics and die in a few years. It didn't make sense that with the billions of dollars being spent on research into many crippling or even fatal conditions, there were no answers for me. Even if the traditional medical community says a disease is incurable and fatal, I think a return to health would seem possible if the right way to treat what is going on in your body is found.

I tried many different kinds of therapies in my search for answers. Most didn't give me the desired results, but this never stopped me from looking for the key to my return to health. I had to follow my gut instinct, which told me there was an answer out there. I was certain there would be a way to conquer this terrible disease. Even if the only confidence in this outcome was mine, it had to be my belief in order to continue going on. The thought that this disease would be deadly to me was unacceptable. It might have been true, but I refused to see it.

I used all my determination and ability to find the right answers in my fight with death. While I was doing research, there was someone out there who was doing his own scientific research. When I found Victor Dyment, his knowledge gave me the correct direction that would take me to complete health. Working with him, came the awareness that he held the answer for my return to health. It wasn't until I started feeling better that I could think about the reality of this incurable and deadly disease. During all my painful symptoms, I wouldn't acknowledge how serious my condition actually was. I had to deny the pain my body felt, although I couldn't deny the disease. In order to attempt to get better, I had to downplay the pain and consequences of what would happen if I didn't find the correct answers.

Through Victor's guidance he was quickly able to reverse the direction my disease was taking. Even though the doctor might be satisfied with a state of remission, that condition would not make me happy. I wanted one hundred percent excellent health. With Victor, that is what I got. And if I can do it, so can others. I am only the first who reversed Systemic Scleroderma. Why? Was I just lucky? Or was I smart enough to realize I had found the right answers that would lead me, and everyone, to perfect health.

Answers do exist for seemingly incurable problems. By sharing my experiences and knowledge, I want to make your journey to health a lot shorter than mine.

Jane M. Parker

# The Journey Begins

*I SAT QUIETLY ON THE doctor's table anxiously listening for his footsteps to make their way down the hall to the examining room. A smiling nurse instructed me to place a thin cotton robe over my naked body. I felt cold in my stillness. My thoughts began to wander. Flashbacks of my illness came to mind.*

*How did it start?*

New Years day, 1995, I awoke with pain in my arm. It was a sharp pain that ran down my forearm from my elbow to my wrist. I thought it must be just a muscle pulled the night before while preparing for my annual New Years Eve party. I enjoyed the preparation and cooking and had been busy all day cutting up onions, red cabbage and potatoes in anticipation of my yearly traditional dinner. The pots and pans became heavy with ingredients and I felt tired going into this holiday season. I might have pushed myself too hard the last few weeks. Maybe the pain would last a day or two and then disappear.

I was an artist, a goldsmith, designing and fabricating my

own jewelry. My work was showing in six galleries across the United States. The busy holiday seasons were always filled with work. Starting in September I tried to put together enough new earrings, necklaces and rings to supply these galleries by mid-November. When my work was in the galleries by Thanksgiving I could take full advantage of the entire winter season. All the pieces that had already been sold needed to be replaced, so I returned to the studio though still bothered by the sharp pains running down my arm. Possibly, the muscles in my arms may have been strained from the milling of gold (flattening it into a sheet) and pulling the gold into wire. On top of my general exhaustion and weakness, I assumed that lifting the heavy pots and pans on New Year's Eve had to be the problem.

Health had never been an issue in my life. I exercised, took vitamins, and found it strange that I should have such pains. At this time I was also undergoing great stress due to a legal problem in my family. I attributed these pains to my generally weakened physical and emotional state, although having always been in touch with my body, I felt something was definitely wrong.

The pains continued, and after ten days I went to my doctor. He thought it was a strain that would heal with time. My work schedule continued although the pain still bothered me. I kept thinking it would stop at any time, but upon awakening each morning there was no relief. Any sort of strain had never lasted for more than a day or two, but this seemed endless.

One night, shortly after my visit to the doctor, a feeling of numbness in my hands woke me up around one o'clock in the morning. It was extremely painful. I rubbed them, shook them trying to restore sensation, and return to sleep. Rest did not come easily as this sensation repeated every hour. After an endless night, the sun finally appeared thru the cracks of my windows.

To my dismay the morning brought no relief. My hands were now beginning to stiffen without let up. Both hands and all my fingers were also becoming swollen. A few more days of this new pain, discomfort and sleepless nights, brought me back once again to my doctor. This time his diagnosis was Carpal Tunnel.

He sent me to an orthopedic doctor who examined my hands, took x-rays and concurred that it was indeed Carpal Tunnel. He prescribed an anti–inflammatory drug, which nauseated me so he switched me to a different drug. He also gave me a splint to wear at night for the numbness. By this time my hands were also getting numb during the day, which resulted in an almost constant use of the splint. The splint offered some relief but within a few weeks I noticed that my fingers continued to swell. I had to remove my wedding band thinking it might get stuck on my finger and would need to be cut off (the ring, not the finger). I didn't know it would take almost four years before I could get that ring back on.

*I felt a shiver run down my body in the cold examining room. Memory… I wish it could play tricks on me like most people believe, but I remembered this journey with clarity.*

*Frustration… oh how I could recall those feelings of being overwhelmed with frustration. Each day spent in the studio, I accomplished less and less. I was used to working quickly and effortlessly, but now my hands were not responding the way they used to. It was more difficult to manipulate the various tools. There was not enough strength in my hands to use the scissors, pliers, tweezers and numerous other pieces of equipment necessary to create my jewelry. I was afraid that if my hands continued to get weaker and more painful I might not be able to work any more. I didn't want to think that this condition was anything other than temporary.*

*My hands remained stiff and swollen. I continued to work in the studio a few days a week, expecting the pains to subside at any time. My work was going slowly and proceeding with great difficulty. My hands did not do the fine work as easily as they used to and they quickly tired.*

*I was even having difficulty with everyday chores at home. My hands were not able to grasp or turn the caps on jars or bottles. I had to go downstairs to the doorman if no one else was home. It might have looked foolish asking for someone to open a cap for me, but there was no way I could do it myself. All of the doormen and workers in the building were very considerate and happy to help me out. It was a very humbling experience, but one that impressed me in the realization of how compassionate people could be.*

Then as now, while sitting and waiting to hear the click of the doctor `s shoes, I knew my life was about to change.

The signs were clear to me. I always worked with my hands. From painting to fashion design, needlepoint design and textile design to finally becoming a jewelry designer. My hands defined my life and that is how I defined myself. Now it was the first part of me to be hurt. Hurt hard, without mercy.

The orthopedic doctor had mentioned that a surgical procedure existed for carpal tunnel patients. My understanding of what the doctor told me was they would cut a nerve in my hand. I didn't like the sound of that. As soon as he said the word "surgery" I wasn't interested, especially if it was on my hands. At the time that direction felt wrong, it was invasive and could be life altering. I was afraid to do anything that might interfere with my life of making jewelry. There had to be other options for me to pursue before taking such a dramatic, dangerous step.

I always was in touch with anything that seemed off in my body. When all of my strange symptoms started, I felt something was definitely wrong and had to be dealt with. Always believing there were higher reasons for everything that happened, whether good or bad, I knew my life was about to change.

My friend Lilyan is a photographer, specializing in children's photography. She had not only taken portraits of my son, Brian, but had also done a few family portraits for me over the years. In February of 1995, I asked Lilyan to take a new portrait of my family. I knew I was changing and would never look the same again, and wanted a record of how I looked before. She gladly obliged, although she tried to reassure me that everything would be fine. I felt deep down, that a whole new part of my life was about to begin.

My search began for a cure. My current doctors were not giving me any kind of answers that sounded accurate to me. Maybe another doctor would have the information I needed to explain what was causing my condition. All directions had to be followed. There must be some alternative method for dealing with my problems. I had to get well to have the use of my hands. I would try anything, go anywhere and would not stop until discovering what was really wrong and how it could be corrected. The Carpal Tunnel diagnosis did not seem correct. The mystery of my body had to be solved and the challenge was taken with a certainty that I would win. My parents had raised me to believe I could succeed in any endeavor I undertook. This was now my battle, and my outcome was never doubted.

Alternative medicine is generally described as medical interventions not commonly taught or used at U.S. schools or hospitals. It is the primary source of health care for approximately 70% of the world's population. The therapies included under the umbrella of alternative or complementary medicine are extremely diverse. Well over 300 modalities fall under this heading, ranging from crystal healing and past life therapy, to those that are complementary to conventional care, such as biofeedback and hypnotherapy. There are also alternative systems of medicine rooted in other cultures, such as Ayurvedic and traditional Chinese medicine. They are grouped together purely because of their exclusion from "conventional" medicine.

While alternative medicine is being turned to more and more, it need not supplant Western scientific medicine. Most people who use alternative medicines use them in conjunction with their conventional care. It is very important not to completely abandon conventional care, but rather to make certain your doctor knows of your use regarding alternative medicine. Because there is no general directory to tell you which alternative practitioner is qualified or how they received their credentials, different therapies vary from practitioner to practitioner. The practitioner should be willing to communicate with your physician.

It was important to find out if anyone understood my symptoms and what they really indicated. It didn't matter to me if it was alternative or conventional western medicine. I wanted help.

For me, the best way to find conventional doctors or alternative practitioners was through the recommendation of my friends. My two good friends Michael and Lilyan were also interested in keeping as healthy as possible and looking into alternative ways of healing our bodies. I trusted their references completely. Among us, we generally heard of who was the best in any given field. Lilyan was seeing a homeopathic doctor and had told me about how much she had been helped. She had felt a tremendous difference in her health. I immediately called Dr. Rebecca Elmaleh and made an appointment. She was booked for the next two months. I felt forlorn but made the first appointment available. Since I had a wait of two months, it gave me some time to look for other options. Lilyan was also under the care of a Kinesiologist. I went on the Internet to research Kinesiology.

Kinesiology is supposedly a method of communicating with another person's nervous system by testing the tension in the muscles. The doctor does manual muscle tests, applying pressure to a person's arm or leg while asking the person to maintain the original position. If the person cannot maintain the test position, the muscle is regarded as inhibited or "weak". The doctor I saw was a chiropractor and he did some manipulation of my body. He then tested me for vitamin weakness, placing a bottle of vitamins in my hand or on my chest and exerting pressure. It was interesting because there was a definite difference in strength when certain vitamins were held in my hand. I bought the vitamins he suggested and made sure to take them every day according to his recommendations. We made another appointment. I thought in the long run he could be helpful, but also felt it would take too long to build up to a full range of vitamins. He wanted to proceed slowly, testing each vitamin as he went. I wanted to do something more... to address the problem immediately. I was willing to take as many vitamins, supplements or drugs as necessary. My feeling was...JUST DO IT NOW!!

Oh when would the doctor please place his hand on the knob and open the door. I grew tired of waiting, tired of remembering but my mind raced ahead.

Memory: After seeing the kinesiologist new problems evolved. My feet became swollen, my joints were becoming stiff, painful, and my legs swelled to twice their normal size. None of my shoes fit. It was painful to walk because the soles of my feet felt tender. I always loved to walk barefoot and never wore shoes in the house. It was very frustrating that this was no longer possible. That was a thing of the past. I had to always wear socks and slippers to have some degree of comfort on the hard floors. I felt the pain and stiffness especially upon awakening. My knees and ankles hurt so much that I had to walk stiff legged for the first half an hour upon rising. I had to buy sneakers a size larger than normal and wear heavy socks to soften the pain. The extra padding and the thick rubber soles of the sneakers were necessary for my feet to be even partially comfortable. Shoes with a leather sole were not an option because they were too uncomfortable. My feet were becoming very cold. I needed the protection the thick rubber soles gave me.

I returned to my internist who took one look at my swollen legs and sent me to a rheumatologist. A new day brought another new doctor. She had never seen me in my normal state so I believe she thought I was exaggerating about the degree to which my legs had swelled. They had swelled to twice their normal size. Even my ankles were much thicker than they had ever been. She herself was somewhat overweight and my new legs were about the same size as hers. She didn't seem too happy about my complaints of fat legs. This was somewhat frustrating, but I let it pass. She did a barrage of blood work, which revealed nothing. At the time it did not occur to me this was just the beginning of being punctured over and over for the next few years. The rheumatologist was not sure what was causing my symptoms. She said I was too old for lupus and decided on a diagnosis of arthritis. Too Old? In this case being called old wasn't too bad, because having lupus was no fun. I wasn't really knowledgeable about that disease but was aware that it was serious. A really serious disease had not been in my thoughts. I had been bothered with psoriasis for 10 years prior to my symptoms but all of the dry skin patches had vanished when the swelling and pain had started. Soon after the skin on my entire body became affected. I lost all the hair on my legs. The hair on my arms was also disappearing. I've never had a lot of hair on my body, and didn't mind not having to shave my legs, but was concerned about these changes. Because of this my diagnosis became psoriatic arthritis.

The doctor suggested we try a drug that was used for Malaria. This treatment sounded very bizarre to me. Even more upsetting was the fact that it could cause problems with your eyesight. People very often became color blind. As an artist, my eyes were my most important part, and color was an integral part of my life experience. There was no way I would even consider this medication. Instead, the doctor prescribed anti-inflammatory drugs. It took time to find one that agreed with me, one that didn't make me sick. The pain remained, but finally there was a diagnosis that seemed to explain all my symptoms. Psoriatic arthritis was as good a diagnosis as any and I accepted it.

Now there was a new diagnosis to go by. I made sure to get copies of all the blood work the doctor performed. I knew I would be seeking other advice and wanted to be able to show any new doctor the current blood test results. Having small veins, it had always been difficult for a doctor or technician to get blood from me. By having copies, hopefully, I wouldn't have to go through the same blood work again. It also would avoid a return to either the rheumatologist or my internist for copies of the lab reports.

I began reading up on arthritis and found there are many different procedures that are possible. The one most logical to me was the use of antibiotics. Dr. Thomas Brown wrote a book called "The Road Back."

Antibiotic therapy is based on the theory that inflammatory rheumatic diseases have an infectious cause, namely mycoplasma and other bacterial L forms. This doctor felt that by using low dose antibiotics, particularly from the tetracycline family, attacks the disease at its source. To me, gathering information became a source of strength within a body rapidly becoming weaker. It kept me positive, hopeful and never did I feel helpless.

I showed my primary care physician all of the research. He agreed to start me on minocycline as recommended in "The Road Back" protocol.

So now I was on anti inflammatory medication and minocycline, which I took twice daily three times a week. I followed this protocol for a few months but saw no difference in my symptoms and stopped the antibiotics. It was time to move on, to look further.

My friend Michael Colberg suggested acupuncture. He had been seeing an acupuncturist and highly recommended her. He had back problems since I had known him and was no stranger to pain. I always looked to him for advice. He tried many different therapies, and if he thought acupuncture might help, I trusted his suggestion. He had tried a few different practitioners and thought the one he recommended was the best. When I told my friends and family about going for acupuncture they knew I must really be desperate. Everyone knew my aversion to needles, so there must be a real problem if I would actually ask someone to stick them in me. I was nervous about going, but was at the point where I would try anything.

At my first appointment the acupuncturist spoke to me at length. Acupuncture's scientific rationale is that inserting needles at specific acupuncture points stimulates the nervous system, releasing chemicals, which either alleviate pain or affects the bodies internal regulating system. Believers feel that meridians, channels of energy, run like energy currents throughout the body. When a blockage in one part of a channel occurs, it impedes the flow in others. Acupuncture removes the blockage and revives the usual flow through the meridians restoring energy balance and helping the body's internal organs with imbalances. Acupuncture supposedly can impact positively on health and wellness, treatment of various medical conditions and prevention of illness. Acupuncture has been acknowledged by the World Health Organization for use in treatment of numerous medical conditions. It can be especially helpful for physical difficulties caused by tension and stress.

She then checked my swollen legs, my hands, my face and neck. She also studied my tongue, and told me acupuncture could be helpful in treating my condition. She assured me that the needles were disposable. There was no need to worry about any risk of infection. When I expressed my fear of needles, she explained that most people feel a minimal pain or no pain at all. The treatments continued for over a month. She also gave me various herbs to take while treating me, which I took religiously. She put most of the needles in my legs and some in my head, but because my legs were so swollen problems occurred with the needles. Wherever inserted there was bleeding. I also felt pain. The acupuncturist was sorry it was not going well and showed surprise with the numerous problems in treating me. I trusted her ability as an acupuncturist. Michael had been to many different people and thought she was the best. I didn't doubt her being able to help other people. As for me I was very uncomfortable during the actual treatment and felt it was not making a difference. I stopped going.

*Will this unknown doctor want to hear my story? Will he wonder why so many tries, why so little success? Here I sat… my skin hurting as if millions of pins were sticking into me and pricking me all over. I needed answers.*

*My body remained cold under the thin cloth of the robe. I continued to wait patiently watching the door, hoping it would soon open. My thoughts continued.*

**May 1995.** Finally, my two months of waiting to see the homeopathic doctor was over. I had always been optimistic at the thought of seeing a new practitioner. Maybe she would be the doctor who would be able to show me the way out of my distress. My feeling was that people who were in the healing business really did want to help people. I would give the person my full cooperation while determining if the treatment was effective or not. I had to believe there would be an answer for my problems, I just had to look hard enough and be able to realize if the advice was good or ineffective.

I walked into a large modern waiting room, signed in and took a seat. It was a space shared by many doctors. While seated my eyes took in large photographs mostly from Africa, reminding me of pictures I had often seen in National Geographic Magazines. On the side tables there were numerous periodicals from World Health organizations.

A young, pretty, French Moroccan doctor came out of her office, smiled at me and introduced herself as Doctor Elmaleh.

Once in her office I showed the doctor copies of my blood work. She did a physical exam and asked me questions no doctor ever asked before; such as the type of weather I enjoyed and what I liked least (storms, hot or cold, thunder, etc.) whether I preferred the mountains to the seashore, which foods I liked, did I favor salt over sweets or vinegar, if I was afraid of snakes, or if I chewed on ice cubes and other seemingly unimportant topics. We discussed my diagnosis (at the time psoriatic arthritis). She prescribed certain remedies and suggested we make another appointment in three months time.

I left and immediately purchased this list of remedies.

Homeopathy is based on the principle that whatever symptoms a substance would cause in overdose, it will help to heal, when given in small, specially prepared doses. Homeopathic remedies can help to stimulate a person's own defense systems, so that the body can heal itself.

The doctor had explained that with homeopathy each person is treated individually, according to his or her symptoms. The homeopathic doctor prescribes a remedy that matches the person's entire range of symptoms, not just the diagnosed disease.

Her advice was sound and I was open to trying it, and diligently taking my remedies did bring relief. At our next appointment she changed a few remedies and I continued to feel quite good. The most important thing for me was that I liked her and felt that homeopathic medicine might help me in the long run.

I took less of the anti-inflammatory drugs because the swelling in my legs and feet began to subside. By October they were almost back to normal. Then November came. The weather got colder and the pains were back.

My family ventured out to watch the Thanksgiving Day parade. We lived on 57th Street and the parade passed by our apartment. I had lived in that neighborhood for the last 20 years and had gone out every year to watch the parade go by. It was always one of the highlights of my Autumn season. It was a cold, rainy day. Instead of being an exciting and happy day, it turned into one of great discomfort. My fingers and toes became very cold and by nightfall I was in great pain, but the pain had shifted. I now felt a strange sensation. My skin hurt. I had never felt anything like this before. It was painful to the touch. It was as if millions of pins were sticking into me and pricking my skin all over. It was now an agony to sit on the couch upholstered in wool. I had to cover it with a soft towel so as not to feel pain. Why was my skin hurting so much?

The skin on my arms became hard and looked shiny aside from being prickly. Once again I returned to my anti-inflammatory drugs. They didn't help. This time nothing helped. It puzzled me to look at my skin. It had developed a strange scaly texture. It's a good thing my sense of humor was still intact, as my husband and son began calling me "lizard girl." Okay...

Through all my miserable discomfort I had continued exercising. Carl was a trainer working at the gym. I liked Carl and thought he was knowledgeable about the safest way to work my body. My uncomfortable condition kept me from continuing with a class so I asked him if he would be my personal trainer and come to my apartment to work with me. I was very happy that he had the time. To my dismay I discovered he understood my painful condition because he himself had arthritis. He had been diagnosed in his early twenties and knew how much stretching and exercise I could safely do. It surprised me that someone so young and strong could be afflicted this way. He said he didn't really discuss it with too many people. If you haven't experienced the joint pains you can't imagine how debilitating it could be. He knew exactly how far he could push me. A certain amount of stretching and exercise is necessary to keep movement in the affected areas. Even if it hurts, you need to keep working on flexibility or else your body really will stiffen up. When the strange symptoms started I didn't want to go back to the same rheumatologist because I didn't feel she had helped me. After telling Carl about the symptoms that now enveloped me, he suggested I go to his rheumatologist, Dr. Mark Horowitz. He said he had asked five different doctors who the best rheumatologist was, and three of them had recommended Dr. Horowitz. Carl had been going to him for a while and thought that he was very knowledgeable as well as a wonderful, caring doctor. There would be a months wait to see him but I made an appointment for the beginning of January. In the meantime Carl and I became a little support group for one another. Though not a complainer I felt a need to tell him of my aches and pains. He exuded sympathy and spoke of his aching joints. During this time he made sure I did a certain amount of stretching. Afterwards he would massage my hands and feet with various arthritis creams he had bought for us to explore. Nothing helped but the massage gave me a great amount of temporary relief. I always looked forward to the time spent with Carl. I was able to relax and let someone I trusted take care of my pain.

*Sitting and waiting; remembering that horrible month of December, the month prickly feelings produced constant pain. Now it was January 1996. An entire year had gone by with no answers. I was in more pain than I had ever been in. My skin was shiny, my hands were stiff, no longer was it possible to work. The cold invaded my very being, freezing my hands and feet.*

*Suddenly I could hear footsteps moving towards my room and saw the door handle turning. I started to feel a renewal of hope in finding answers for my condition. Maybe this was the doctor who could really help me. After hearing from Carl how wonderful he was, I had to feel totally optimistic about my future. Finally the doctor had arrived.*

He was a tall man. I thought his head could almost touch the low ceiling of the examining room. Dr. Horowitz greeted me with a handshake and a smile. His face was kind, his manner unassuming. I didn't have to say a word because he took one look at me and said I definitely had a disease called Scleroderma. I was right to have felt optimistic. As soon as he looked at me he was able to give me a name for my condition. When I told him of other diagnoses, he shook his head. He said I definitely did not have arthritis and asked if the anti-inflammatory drugs had helped. When I told him they hadn't he wasn't surprised. It was a big relief that he was able to look at me and tell me exactly what was wrong with me. He was the first doctor who before any testing could give me a certain diagnosis. Why was he the only one? And what was this disease called Scleroderma? Dr. Horowitz explained that I had visible symptoms of this illness. He knew this because he had done his fellowship with Dr. Harry Spiera, who is an acknowledged Scleroderma expert. This had allowed him the opportunity to see many cases of Scleroderma and gain experience with the disease. My hope in him was renewed by this information.

I had never heard of Scleroderma before. It was never mentioned by any of the other doctors. Dr. Horowitz explained exactly what Scleroderma was and gave me a booklet about it. He wanted to draw blood from me for a series of tests. I told him no one could get blood from me. He smiled and said he was good at it. He never trusted a technician but always drew the blood himself because he didn't want to put his patients through any excess discomfort. I was very impressed that he was able to draw blood from my almost nonexistent veins. He also suggested I do a series of tests for my heart, lungs, and an upper GI to make sure that my esophagus had not been affected.

I was overjoyed at having finally found a doctor who was able to recognize what was wrong with me. I had confidence in his ability to help me.

**SCLERODERMA:** Scleroderma, also called progressive systemic sclerosis, is one of the least known disorders in the family of rheumatic diseases. Rheumatic diseases affect joints, muscles and connective tissues of the body. The word scleroderma means "hard skin". There are actually two kinds of Scleroderma: localized or limited, and systemic or generalized.

In localized Scleroderma, changes occur only in limited parts of the body, such as the skin, muscles or bones, but not in the internal organs. This kind is relatively mild. People who have localized disease usually do not develop Systemic Scleroderma. Systemic Scleroderma causes changes in the connective tissue in many parts of the body. It may show up not only in the skin but also in many internal body parts, including the blood vessels, the digestive system (esophagus, stomach and bowels), the lungs, kidneys, muscles and joints. Changes in the connective tissue may affect the functions of any of these body parts. Scleroderma differs from person to person. One who has the systemic form of the disease may have one or more body parts affected to different degrees. It's hard to predict how the disease will develop in each individual.

The connective tissue cells of people who have this disease produce too much of a protein called collagen. In Scleroderma this excess collagen is deposited in the skin and body organs. This may cause thickening and hardening of the skin.

Scleroderma is referred to as a rheumatic autoimmune disease. Autoimmune is the process whereby the immune system mistakenly recognizes the body's own protein as foreign invaders and begins producing antibodies that attack healthy cells and tissue causing a variety of diseases. The immune system normally works to defend the body against infections by identifying and eliminating invading viruses, bacteria and other disease causing microbes. But in people with autoimmune disorders, the body turns on itself. The immune system mistakenly attacks other cells, tissues and organs. Doctors and scientists do not fully understand the factors that may trigger autoimmune diseases. Scleroderma can occur in people of any age, race or sex, but it occurs most commonly in young or middle-aged women between the ages of 25 and 55. Women are affected two to three times more often than men.

Dr. Horowitz suggested treatment begin immediately. The most effective drug in treating this disease is called Penicillamine. Scleroderma is the production of excess collagen, and Penicillamine interferes with this production thereby making it less efficient. He also said I would need blood tests once a month and my urine tested for protein. He gave me information about the drug and its side effects. Another appointment was made for me when all of the test results would be available.

Upon returning home I went on the Internet to look up Scleroderma. What I read was a shock to me. In 1996, all reports had doctors basically agreeing that you had from two to seven years to live from the time of diagnosis. There was no way I was going to accept a death sentence like that.

People read about diseases and believe it when "the experts" say there is no reversal or relief. I read the same reports and didn't care what they said; I would search for the information that would ultimately give me answers. I never believed I would die. Not for one minute did I believe it...me, never. It was simply not possible, and totally unacceptable. I would destroy this killer disease, become victorious in this battle with death. Believing the doomsayers is for other people. I rejected words of hopelessness. I would find my own answers and disprove the negative theories floating in cyberspace. Let others accept what they are told – I don't have to!!! There are those who might say it is living in denial, or being delusional, but for me there was never a doubt in my mind that I would once again be totally healthy. This illness invaded my body but could not invade my spirit. My vision had always been a totally optimistic one about life and what it held for me in the future. This would only be a momentary setback in the adventure that was my life.

I immediately called Dr. Elmaleh and told her the diagnosis. I wanted her opinion about the Penicillamine, and if she thought it was worth the side effects. I needed to know what to do. We spoke for a long time about the condition and the drug. Her final suggestion was to see if there was a time frame for taking the drug and if there were any medical alternatives. She suggested giving it a try provided I was closely supervised. I could always stop taking it if the results didn't please me.

I returned with my husband for a second visit with Dr. Horowitz. He had his own questions to ask and wanted to make sure I didn't forget anything that was said. I also needed the extra support while listening to my test results. We were both relieved to learn there was no internal involvement. Dr. Horowitz felt we were catching the disease early on and the best way to keep the Scleroderma from getting any worse was to begin the Penicillamine immediately. I began the medication at a low dosage of 150 mg., remained on that dosage for two weeks and returned for another blood test. When he saw that there had been no side effects he increased the dosage. We continued the two week routine, raising the dosage each time until after three months I reached full dosage of 750 mg. a day. Blood work was done every two weeks, and luckily there were no side effects from the drug. For the first time I was confident help had arrived, and let my friends know that life appeared to be under control.

My good friend Michael knew someone who also had Scleroderma. He gave me advice about things I might not have thought twice about. Mostly everyday activities, such as reaching into the refrigerator or the freezer had to be done quickly. I had to always be aware of my hands, taking care of them by not allowing the cold to make them worse. Life needed to continue without any new interruptions because I didn't want my disease to affect my son Brian.

My thoughts turned to memory. To a time my son at five

years old discovered ice- skating. It was a sport that had always given me pleasure and my time with Brian on the ice brought the two of us lots of joy and laughter. Then the pain arrived and I could no longer wear my skates. My feet were in agony from the cold ice and the tightness of the ice skates. I could vividly see myself hobbling around after removing the skates until my feet got used to my shoes again. But still we continued to skate for a few more weeks until I physically could not stand it anymore. I knew that Brian was really enjoying his time on the ice, and didn't want him to stop because of my pain, but from that time on he only went skating on week-ends when his father could take him.

When we reached the full dosage Dr. Horowitz continued the blood tests, but only once a month to make sure that nothing had changed in my reactions. Dr. Horowitz now included a medicine to avoid high blood pressure. Penicillamine can affect your kidneys, and create this new condition. My blood pressure was always on the low side. This new medicine brought with it more than my usual exhaustion so he agreed I should stop taking it. He then made an appointment for me with Dr. Spiera; Chief of Rheumatology at Mount Sinai Hospital in New York City. Dr. Spiera confirmed the diagnosis.

"Once Scleroderma was thought of as a terminal illness," Dr. Spiera said, "But now with the treatment and therapies available, Scleroderma is considered a chronic illness. There is every expectation that the majority of patients can live with the illness for many years."

He didn't give me a number and I was afraid to ask. For some people, two years is many. For me, fifty years would not be enough. He went on to say that the Scleroderma could be maintained at this level by using the Penicillamine.

"I don't want to keep the disease at this level," was my retort... "I want to return to my old, healthy self."

He looked at me and said nothing, but I knew he held no hope for me to reverse my condition.

A month later my face was beginning to tighten and it became hard to open my mouth wide. The disease was progressing quickly and I was concerned, upset and angered by my worsening condition. The doctor, (Dr. Horowitz) had told me we had caught the disease at an early stage, so why was this happening? I knew there would be no giving up. Instead my resolve to be well became stronger. I even told the doctor I was going to be totally healthy. Dr. Horowitz didn't believe I recognized the severity of my disease, but it didn't matter what he thought. My goal was to return to health, though no one had ever reversed this disease before.

*Sitting on my living room couch, my gaze rested on the shapes the sun made on the Oriental rug. I had a home, a family and Scleroderma. My thoughts focused on the disease.*

I was surprised to learn that approximately twenty percent of the U.S. population suffers from autoimmune related diseases. Of these, 75 percent are women. The autoimmune diseases are the most difficult to diagnose, and most physically and emotionally painful diseases facing people today. My own experience showed me how painful this disease could be. It is incredible to me how many people suffer from Scleroderma and have no hope. In many cases they don't even have a name for all these symptoms that are causing them so much suffering. They can feel that there is no hope for them to live a pain free existence. NO HOPE. They can't even find out if they have a real illness or it is something emotional. In many cases, symptoms develop gradually over a period of years and are so subtle you may not notice them. And when a woman does seek medical attention, a woman's complaints may not be taken seriously. In one study, more than 65 percent of patients in the early stages of their illness were labeled hypochondriacs, according to the American Autoimmune -Related Diseases Association (AARDA). Scleroderma is primarily a disease in women, and a majority of primary care physicians are men and not always familiar with the disease known as Scleroderma. Given this breakdown, it becomes easy for the men doctors to dismiss the various symptoms as emotional responses. If the doctor has not seen other patients who actually have Scleroderma, the numerous and often seemingly unrelated symptoms can point to other diagnoses.

*I was now enduring skin changes, a hardening and thickening of my skin, especially on the hands, arms and face. I knew it was possible to get ulcers on your fingers. There can be a decrease in hair over the affected area. The quality of my hair had definitely changed. I not only lost hair on my body, but the hair on my head was now lifeless and thinner. No conditioner or shampoo could change this. I had tried them all. There was also a noticeable change in my skin color. It became slightly darker with a yellow cast I never had before. My face was an entirely different color. As I sat there feeling the rays from the sun that enveloped my apartment, I knew I would look at myself in the mirror only if necessary so as not to be discouraged or deterred from my journey to health.*

When I told my mother about the diagnosis of Scleroderma, there was no mention of only having two to seven years to live. I did not want to worry my parents, knowing this death sentence would not apply to me. They didn't need to know that this disease was deadly. There seemed to be no hope for a person diagnosed with Scleroderma. I didn't want to put any added worry on them. My parents were positive people and believed with proper knowledge everything can be made better, so it did not surprise me when my mother began her own research into what I should do. She has always been a firm believer in vitamins, proper nutrition and doing anything and everything to improve your health. She constantly read books and magazines on health, and tuned in to hear health orientated radio programs. On one occasion she heard Dr. Mitchell Gaynor speak. He had written a book called "Healing Essence." This book was about healing cancer patients. He basically believes the disease to be stress related. My mother believed that stress could also have been an influence on my condition. After reading his book, it seemed that he had ideas that might be beneficial to me. I suspected that stress reduction and visualization could help, and called Dr. Gaynor to make an appointment. I spoke to his receptionist, explaining about my Scleroderma. I briefly told her my background and described the effects of this autoimmune disease on my body. I continued by saying that after reading his book, it seemed the direction of Dr. Gaynor's research could just as easily apply to my disease. Even though he only worked with cancer patients, it might be interesting for him to try his ideas on a different disease. Maybe he could use his knowledge to help a whole different group of patients. There was no hope for Scleroderma. Let's see what he could do with me.

The receptionist informed me he had a waiting period of six months for new patients. He wasn't even booking too many new appointments because he had such a large practice already. She was very nice and had listened to everything I had to say and told me she would talk to Dr. Gaynor and get back to me. I was thrilled when she called me back the next day, saying he had agreed to see me. We set up an appointment for three days later.

Dr. Gaynor believes illness is a manifestation of many things and for the most part, Western medicine has just looked at the illness itself. He thinks that is only one part of the problem. He tries to identify the causes behind the manifestation and deal with as many of those causes as possible. He also looks at the emotional factors, such as trauma or stress leading into the disease. There are also environmental factors to take into consideration.

Dr. Gaynor approached everything in an integrative manner, by looking at people's diet, environment, and what trauma they might be carrying in their bodies and unconscious. Guided imagery and meditation can change a patient's perspective by helping to enhance their self-image and see themselves in a more positive light. My interpretation of this was to figure out where the stress came from that brought me to the point of getting sick. After coming to terms with the fact that I did have a disease, I had to realize how this disease had changed my life and how my thought patterns had affected me up until that time. I then had to work with these facts to turn my life and my health around. My entire life had been disrupted and my way of thinking had to be changed.

At our first appointment, I brought copies of all of my blood work and lab results from all the tests that had been done. Dr. Gaynor now had my diagnosis and test results, so it was easy to take the next step. He gave me a booklet about diet and a list of supplements to take. At this first meeting with Dr. Gaynor, I felt good about him and his outlook on dealing with life.

Dr. Gaynor had a series of meditation tapes that he encouraged me to use. He spoke on each tape, first relaxing you, than covering different aspects of dealing with your ailment. One tape concerned itself with facing the fear of having a disease. Other tapes helped you come to terms with the changes in your life as a result of your disease. Another dealt with emotional issues. I believed I was already dealing with all the emotional aspects. I wasn't depressed, but always was optimistic and looking forward. I had come to terms with turning around my entire life, knowing my life was about to change from the moment my hands stopped working properly. Now I would have to deal with the world, with all sorts of people, different doctors, healers, whatever it took. I had always enjoyed my isolation, but this was no longer possible. It was now necessary for me to change my life in order to be well. In the past I lived exactly as I pleased; secluded with special friends who encouraged my choices both in life and work, but now the choices were no longer mine. Although I had stopped looking in the mirror, I always glanced at the picture Lilyan had taken, vowing to return to what I once was, though the outcome was unclear. Would my body ever be the same as it was? In my heart my hopes were high. I knew my old life was over. Everything would have to be done differently. But for now, I just needed to deal with the pain.

I bought the series of Dr. Gaynor's meditation tapes determined to listen in the morning and before bed at night. At this time, as in the past, I felt a great deal of pain and aching in my joints, pain that was hard to ignore. My shoulders and arms were especially affected. My knees and ankles had also begun to stiffen up. I was uncomfortable in just about any position, whether standing up, sitting or lying down. This made it difficult to find a comfortable position to begin my meditation. The tapes were each around 20 minutes long. I had to get past the pain in order to control it. At first it was very hard sitting or lying in pain and trying not to hurt. To help me I imagined a red light across the room to focus on. For me, the red was an indication of the pain I was suffering. My thought was that by placing the pain outside my body all the red pain on the inside would soon follow. The tapes helped because it forced me to focus outside myself allowing me to feel more in control of the pain. As I was able to relax, so did the hurting.

After seeing Dr. Gaynor and trying to meditate on my own, he suggested a therapist/ healer. He asked me to keep in touch and let him know the results. I went to this therapist to help me with his relaxation and meditation techniques. We also worked on guided imagery to try and stop the collagen from increasing. She would walk me through various scenarios to help me come to a relaxed state. In one of these images she asked me to imagine myself at the beach. I do not like the ocean so she tried to have me visualize a lake. Suggesting she stay away from water, she easily switched to mountain settings for my mind wanderings. Many times, she played tapes of guided imagery that she had gotten at various lectures she had attended in her learning experience. Many of the tapes were helpful. Some were annoying. There was one favorite image she created for me, that had me imagine my feet spreading wide apart and roots began coming down my legs through my feet and into the ground. At the same time the top of my head was opening up to the universe above me. This higher energy ran down into my body and then back up out of my head washing down the outside of my body. While my feet grounded my body in the earth, the universe was washing healthy energy into me from above. I found this experience both relaxing and energizing at the same time. I asked if she would record this imagery for me to use at home. She seemed somewhat surprised that I preferred this to the tapes that other people had done. She agreed and made me a tape of her telling this story. This imagery was the most helpful to me.

She ended each session with a period of therapeutic touch.

Dennis Gersten, M.D., a San Diego psychiatrist has said, "Imagery is the language that the mind uses to communicate with the body. You can't talk to a wart and say the words, "Hey, go away," because that is not the language that the brain uses to communicate with the body. You need to imagine the wart and see it shrinking. Imagery is the biological connection between the mind and body." Most people have thousands of thoughts and images going through their minds each day. At least half of those thoughts are negative. A steady dose of worry and other negative images can alter your physiology and make you more susceptible to many ailments of all kinds. If you can learn to direct and control the images in your head, you can help your body heal itself.

Dr. Rossman says, "The imagination is like a spirited, powerful horse. If it's untamed, it can be dangerous and run you over. But if you learn to use your imagination in a way that is purposeful and directed, it can be a tremendously powerful vehicle to get you where you want to go." In my case I wanted to ride that powerful horse to better health.

The belief that imagination can help cure your ills isn't a new one. Imagery has been considered a healing tool in all of the world's cultures and is an integral part of many religions. Navajo Indians, for example, practice an elaborate form of imagery that encourages a person to "see" himself as healthy. Ancient Egyptians and Greeks believed that images release spirits in the brain that arouse the heart and other parts of the body. How imagery works its wonders in the body is still a mystery. Some evidence suggests, however, that the brain reacts the same way to an imagined sensation as to a real one. If you can learn to use the images in your mind instead of letting them flow over you with no direction, they can have a positive, long-term effect on your health and well-being.

For me the best images are the ones I conjured up for myself. I tried to imagine little soldiers in white suits with torches breaking apart the collagen and stopping new production from occurring.

I also made a point of taking 20 minutes every morning and every night to listen to Dr. Gaynor's tapes. It was difficult at first to actually relax enough to listen to the tapes. The aching of my entire body was hard to ignore. My arms and legs were the most uncomfortable. My son had to get used to the idea that he couldn't interrupt me during my meditation time. When I saw that the tapes did make a difference and were helping me control the pain, my meditations and guided imagery were continued religiously. I went to the therapist once a week for a few months. There were certain meditations and imagery that were helping me the most and I became confident that I could continue doing them on my own. There was no longer a need to spend the extra time and money on that particular aspect of my healing.

My guided imagery therapist had studied with a healer named Gary Elder. He was living in Italy but came to the U.S. on a regular basis. She suggested I see him. I called and left a message, but he wasn't planning on being in the States right away. In the past I had seen a world famous healer and formed a positive relationship with him. Our original meetings were because of my interest in alternative therapies, even though there was nothing particularly wrong with me. At the time of our visits I was happy to get any extra help in order to continue being healthy. I believed he had infused me with positive energy. In the fifteen years of seeing him, I was never sick. After looking for him when diagnosed with Scleroderma he was nowhere to be found. I was hoping Gary Elder could do the same. There had been no need for me to find a healer up until that time. I hadn't heard any recommendations about people doing healing. At least not from anyone whose opinion I valued. Michael and Lilyan were the only ones trusted for that kind of evaluation. They would always hear about different psychics, therapists and healers. They knew how particular I was and wouldn't refer me to anyone who wasn't real. They knew I had a problem with anyone who was trying to pull one over on unsuspecting people. Most healers and psychics I had met were into an ego trip. The most important thing should be the power they control, a misplaced or overblown ego on their part didn't impress me. When the therapist told me about Gary Elder, it was the first I had heard of any healer in a long time. He supposedly had a big reputation in Europe. I was very eager to meet Gary, although didn't feel the therapist had very much of a healing power herself. When she used therapeutic touch on me, it felt nice but not especially powerful. I always liked any kind of energy work or massage so it was fine. Hopefully a healer that was teaching other people how to tap into their innate healing abilities would be able to actually heal me, even if his student couldn't do the job. I felt disappointed that there would be a few weeks until he returned to New York. I wasn't going to sit around doing nothing until then, and continued my search. I was open to any new ideas that might help me.

I had still been trying to walk around as much as possible, but was limited by my pains. In looking back I realized how easy everything had once been. Living in a great location in the City, it was easy to walk almost everywhere. I could take my son to Central Park and walk along Fifth Avenue at anytime. Now I had too much pain to enjoy what was so close to me. As the disease developed, it took me longer to get to my destination. The same distance would take me twice as long. Eventually the pain became too intense. I would have to take a bus, or if I were really in a rush, I'd take a taxi. With the traffic in the city, it was now taking me longer to do what had always been accomplished so easily. It was also costing me for all this slower transportation. It was getting very frustrating. I couldn't imagine my condition getting worse. It was becoming more difficult for me to get around. Everything had been so easy for me before. I realized how lucky I had been to be able to go anywhere, do anything without giving it a second thought. Now everything was an effort.

In May we went to Florida on vacation. I brought my tapes and was taking all the supplements that Dr. Gaynor had recommended along with the Penicillamine. I stopped the homeopathic remedies. Enough was enough. The thought of getting away, leaving my everyday existence and being in new surroundings filled me with renewed energy, renewed hope. Wanting so much to feel healthy, I didn't watch my diet, indulging in bacon and eggs, along with plenty of meat and dairy. This indulgence plus the hot, sticky climate of Florida brought on more pain and discomfort then ever before. My skin once again felt prickly; my joints ached more and became even stiffer. Though I was listening to Dr. Gaynor's tapes religiously, I was a mess. My arms would go only as high as shoulder level, not above my head, making it difficult to get dressed and undressed. I had to buy new t-shirts a size larger than usual. In order to take the shirt off, I needed to hold the edge of a sleeve with my opposite hand, than pull my elbow down to get it out of the shirt from the bottom. I proceeded to do the same with the other sleeve. When both my arms were free it could be pulled over my head by bending over. My fingers could no longer manipulate buttons in and out of those small holes so I had to buy new shirts and jeans that only had snaps. There was no winning because of my decreasing ability to raise my arms. Everything once taken for granted as effortless now only made me acutely aware of motion; motion I could no longer manage. I was becoming more and more frustrated. Who would have thought about all the arm movements one makes without even thinking about it. I was now aware of every movement that I couldn't do. My ears were pierced and I had a large collection of earrings that I had made. My hands were getting more stiff and tired, making it difficult to hold the small earrings. The backs were almost impossible to pick up and I couldn't manipulate them onto the back of the post. I couldn't work any of the clasps on my necklaces. The few pieces of jewelry brought along on the trip were put away in my bag. My frustration was intensifying.

Upon returning home I called Dr. Elmaleh and described my discomfort. She thought it might be related to my diet, particularly dairy products, and recommended I see the nutritionist working out of her office. When Dr. Elmaleh said it might be dairy, it came as a real shock. I once again had that sinking feeling of deprivation. All the foods, the hamburgers, bacon and eggs, pancakes with butter, and all the dairy products I spent a lifetime enjoying, would most probably be taken away from me.

Nevertheless I called to make an appointment with the nutritionist, Dr. Shari Lieberman, and told her of my illness. She wanted to research Scleroderma before my arrival. When the day of my appointment arrived, a perky lady with lots of energy and a warm, friendly manner showed me into her office. Dr. Lieberman told me the trouble with treating Scleroderma is that there is little research done on the disease, so she included research on lupus and multiple sclerosis. I was impressed with the amount of information she had gathered before our first meeting. She explained that our immune system is a complex system of blood cells and special proteins acting together to defend us from harm. Improving our immune defense system is the main incentive behind modern preventive medicine because it protects us in so many important ways. This system, though powerful, is extremely delicate, its parts totally interdependent upon one another. If any one aspect is compromised, we open ourselves up to many diseases.

As suspected, she suggested I totally change my eating habits, taking me off all dairy products, refined sugar, oils and red meat. She said that red meat has a variety of hormones and antibiotics from the way the animal had been fed, and believed that more vegetarian food would be beneficial. She also advised the avoidance of foods that are low in nutrients and high in harmful substances like salt and sugar. I could still eat fish and chicken, and organic foods whenever possible. I continued to have my cup of coffee in the morning, although now drinking organic coffee. Feeling deprived of so many foods, she couldn't deny me my daily cup of coffee. There had been a lot of frustration in my morning ritual already. I always enjoyed cappuccino in the morning. My cousins had gone to Italy in the early 1970's and brought me back a machine. That was before it was popular but I was hooked. By the early 80's I had a new cappuccino maker. The espresso came out by lifting a handle and pressing down to get the water to go through the grounds. It never felt as if I were using excessive strength to work it. Now I needed two hands to work the lever, but then the entire machine would lift up. I didn't realize I had been holding the machine down with my left hand and working the pump with my right. I had to get a regular coffee machine that had a milk steamer on the side. It wasn't as good as a real cappuccino machine but it had to do. Now I had to change my morning coffee yet again, and started using soy milk in my coffee. (Coffee is obviously a big part of my life.) At first it was a shock to my taste buds, but I quickly got used to the taste. The benefits to my health were certainly worth giving up milk in my coffee. Dr. Lieberman also added a long list of vitamins and supplements to take each day. Then she asked me something new.

"Do you have many fillings in your teeth?"

Her question surprised me.

"Do I have fillings!!" (I must have had about 30 of them, starting from the time I was a little girl.)

"Every one of my clients with an autoimmune disease responds to that question in the same way."

She continued to explain the importance of removing

amalgam fillings, and gave me the name of a dentist who specialized in just that. I took the information but wasn't sure about dealing with extensive dental work just yet. I wasted no time in beginning the diet restrictions and taking the vitamin supplements. The results were amazing to me.

With this new diet regime in place my skin was no longer prickly and I felt less pain, but after a few weeks of being good I couldn't resist a slice of pizza. Within fifteen minutes my arms began to tingle. That was it for me. This proved to me that diet did make a difference, but when I relayed my new information to Dr. Horowitz, he was only mildly interested. I had always told him about all my alternative processes. He listened patiently, but felt any good results were because of the Penicillamine. I knew better.

During the next few months I felt healthier. I took long walks in the early morning hours, loving the stillness of the city and particularly the beauty of Central Park. During these interludes emotions surfaced, emotions held in check because I needed to be strong, steadfast to deal with my illness. Walking alone through the wonders of nature, I cried out with frustration at all that was happening to me. I cried in understanding what I was trying to accomplish by myself. Most people do the crying when contracting symptoms, then cry again when receiving the dreaded diagnosis. I knew I had to be strong, positive and refused to allow myself to be run over by life. I was still optimistic. I had found people who really were trying to help me. People who are in touch with themselves at the deepest level, know they have some control over their lives. Nothing remains the same, even nature changes. I looked around me, at the tall trees, the dark dirt, the green grass and thanked God I was alive.

Suddenly there were news programs on television about

removing amalgam fillings from teeth and how this process related to autoimmune diseases. More and more information about the effects of mercury was now available. Although these fillings are commonly called silver fillings because they look silver for the first few days of the eight to twelve years they survive in the average human head, mercury fillings is the more accurate label.

Tales of mercury's damaging effects date to ancient Roman and Spanish history, when imprisoned slaves working in mercury mines suffered from acute symptoms of fatigue and various pains on their first day in the mines. As time passed, they developed other common symptoms of mercury poisoning. These included lesions of the nervous system with signs of moodiness, tremors and other mental disturbances. These slaves were condemned to death in the mines because they eventually wasted away in the terminal stages of mercury poisoning. A more recent example of mercury's dangers comes from the British hat-making industry of the late nineteenth century. At the time, the expression "mad as a hatter" characterized workers who used mercury compounds in the shaping of felt hats. The workers exhibited unusual shyness, mood swings and a dwindling intellect, all symptoms of severe mental retardation. These dangers were recognized for three-quarters of a century before the use of mercury in the U.S. hat –making industry was banned in 1941. An interesting historical note is that the common term for mercury in Germany in those years was "quick silver." The German pronunciation for "quick" is "quack." Thus, those dentists who used mercury were called "quacks."

After doing research on the effects of mercury toxicity, and seeing a report on amalgam removal on a local news program, my husband encouraged me to have the work done. I called Dr. Roger Gershon and was impressed at the amount of time he took to speak with me. He seemed nice, knowledgeable and forthcoming with information. He explained he worked on many people with autoimmune diseases and the results amazed him. I felt confident that he was the right dentist to work on me. After speaking to him on the phone for over 20 minutes we set up an appointment. At my first appointment with Dr. Gershon, he checked my teeth to see how many fillings needed to be changed. There were so many that he wanted to do my mouth one section at a time. This would take four sessions. The first step was a complete blood work up through a special lab in Colorado. I asked Dr. Horowitz to draw my blood for the tests, since he was the only one who could easily get the blood out of me. He was still doing blood tests once a month. All the work might as well be done at the same time, so my insurance could cover part of it anyway. I told Dr. Horowitz about having all my dental work changed. He thought I was putting myself through a lot. He was skeptical but knew that whatever I had done so far had been working. Kindly, he never discouraged me.

**December 1996 Dr. Gershon:** At my next appointment he explained it was important that the patient, the dentist and his assistant be protected from the mercury vapor. To keep the fumes from being inhaled, we all put on oxygen masks. Dr. Gershon made a rubber dam to cover the inside of my mouth with only an opening for the teeth he worked on. This consisted of a thin piece of rubber that was held in place by a metal brace. He cut a small hole in the rubber and fit it over the tooth he worked on leaving only that area exposed. He used a lot of water continually flushing out the area as he worked. When he removed the fillings he utilized a machine to measure the mercury vapor in the cavity, and continued to flush it out until the levels were low enough to put in the new filling.

First he worked on the upper left side of my mouth. This took approximately an hour and a half. It was difficult because my mouth couldn't open very wide. This was one of the effects of the Scleroderma. My mouth had become tighter since my visit with Dr. Spiera. He had said my condition would remain at the same level, but now my mouth was worse. It would not open wide enough to eat a sandwich, even a thin sandwich was difficult. Aside from the discomfort of the dental work there was the extra pain on the sides of my mouth from the dentist poking his hands and equipment in there. Sitting so long in one position while he worked also brought aching to my back and legs. Even with all the discomfort, I felt I was definitely doing the right thing. There were three more sessions over the course of the next few months before all was completed, over thirty fillings in all, plus a large inlay of holistic gold, the only one the lab reported I wasn't allergic to. By the time Dr. Gershon finished his work the skin on my face had softened enough so that my mouth could once again open wide, but this did not eliminate all my eating problems. Before the work, my mouth could not close around a straw tightly enough to allow me enough suction power. After the dental work it was easier to use a straw. The upper GI series were always very difficult. I had to stand up in front of the x-ray equipment and drink the liquid that would show up on the screen. Of course this was done through a straw. It took a long time to finish the test because of all my maneuvering to get the liquid down. Happily no internal involvement had been found. The last test became much easier because my mouth was working more efficiently.

I still had trouble holding a glass because my hand wouldn't close around it, needing to use both hands to maneuver it to my mouth. If the beverage was cold my hands instantly began to freeze.

In the past I had lost the hair on my arms, then my skin

hardened, but by my last session with Dr. Gershon there was hair growing on my left arm. Both the dentist and myself were thrilled. I showed Dr. Horowitz the new hair and how my face had now softened. He agreed that having my fillings changed definitely made a difference. He said he would never have suggested it but that it certainly had helped.

Considering the positive results received by doing the dental work, I was surprised when Dr. Gershon said he could not legally recommend it. As a dentist he isn't allowed to recommend removing amalgam fillings for any reason other than aesthetic. He is only permitted to say that your mouth would look better with white fillings, but not that it is healthier. The ADA does not admit there is anything wrong with amalgam, even though it contains mercury. There are standards of the amount of mercury allowed, though it is well known that high levels of mercury is dangerous to your health. Still dentists are encouraged to primarily use amalgam, and though removing the amalgam helped my condition enormously, it was up to me to do the research and find the right doctor to do the work.

Dr. Gershon suggested that I also go for Chelation therapy. This therapy detoxifies the body by removing heavy metals such as lead, mercury, aluminum, cadmium, and many more. He believed that undergoing this procedure would remove any metals that might remain in my body. After doing some research, it seemed it could only be done through the veins. Having very small veins, it was always difficult for most technicians to draw blood, much less be hooked up on a needle for an hour at a time. I spoke to the doctor recommended by Dr. Gershon, the specialist in Chelation therapy. My impression of him was someone who liked publicity and an admiring list of patients. He charged more than most other doctors and showed neither sympathy nor compassion.

When I inquired about the possibility of oral chelation instead of being hooked up to a machine through a needle, he answered in the negative saying it had to be done intravenously, but reassured me his technicians would have no problems. I decided to give him a chance and see if this therapy could really help continue my improvement that the dental work had started. The first step was to submit to a barrage of tests, even though many seemed unnecessary. In trying to speak with the doctor again, he made himself inaccessible. I was told in no uncertain terms that it was necessary to take all the tests before making another appointment. He had a nutritionist in the office and a consultation was scheduled. This was someone who never heard of Scleroderma. I told her about my work with Dr. Lieberman and what she had told me, showing her the list of vitamins and supplements I'd been taking. She appeared interested and charged me one hundred twenty five dollars. There was also blood work to be done. The doctor's assistant insisted he could do it, though I explained how difficult it was. My imploring made no impression so I decided to let him try. Even if it hurt me, I wanted to make a point. The technician tried one arm. Nothing. He tried the other arm. Nothing. He tried both my hands. Nothing. He even attempted to draw blood from my feet. By this time I was in tears. The other technicians and nurses in the room watched his failure in astonishment. Through my tears, I cried out, "Do you believe me now? You can't do it." He wasn't very pleased having failed so miserably, but unfortunately he was one of the people I had to contact in the office for information. Needless to say, he never returned my calls.

The tests that were performed showed no metal residues in my body. They did a hair analysis, which came up negative and also a patch test for copper and mercury that also had negative results. There was one liver function test that involved a twenty-four hour urine test along with a few vials of drawn blood. In reading the information that came with the package, it said the tests could be done without blood work. I called the doctor's office and was told by one of his assistants that the entire test had to be done as directed. Upon doing more research, came the discovery that Penicillamine is used as a chelation agent and given as part of the liver test. Once again I called the office to remind them of the fact that I had been taking Penicillamine for the last year. It made no impression. Each patient was treated the same, no matter what was wrong.

Since they had failed to attain any blood from me, the doctor agreed to allow someone outside his office to do a few of the tests. I asked Dr. Horowitz to do some of the blood work for the chelation tests. Dr. Horowitz wanted to know what the tests were for but the other doctor's office would not respond to his questions. One of the tests involved a measles vaccine, and no one could explain why. There was no speaking to the main doctor and his assistant would not return my calls. I concluded it was best to rely on my gut feelings concerning both the doctor and the treatment. The chelation was not for me, but I needed to express my anger directly to the doctor. Upon calling his office, the receptionist told me there would be no appointment with the doctor until all required tests were completed. Knowing I would not waste my time or money on what he asked for, I waited a few days, then telephoned claiming to have the test results. An appointment was finally made. Seeing the doctor helped my rage bubble over and surface. I refused to be seated, preferring to stand while he sat behind his massive desk. Then proceeded to tell him how his assistant had punctured me all over with no blood taken, and ranted on about the twenty-four hour test with the Penicillamine. I continued by exclaiming he had a know nothing nutritionist, and finished by announcing my outrage at the entire way he conducted business. He responded with silence. When he finally spoke it was to calmly ask when I'd be ready to make an appointment for the chelation treatments. "Unbelievable," I thought, and walked out. The receptionist stopped me, wanting four hundred dollars for the fifteen minutes spent telling the doctor what I thought of him. Though always prompt paying my bills, this time my response was easy... "Send me the bill." I never heard from him again.

There weren't too many practitioners who got me that angry. It always infuriates me when someone tries to take advantage of another person. I get especially incensed when these people give misleading information to people who are seriously ill and often believe what is told to them by these uncaring and self-centered egotists. I was dealing with a seemingly incurable disease but was not about to let someone get away with telling me that by paying him all this money, he would help me. With his attitude, he could create more damage in people who came to him with hope for relief. If they believed he had answers, they might not look any further and get even sicker. Even if I was just one person calling him out on his disservice to people, I had to tell him my feelings. He probably wouldn't change in trying to take advantage of people, but maybe he would think twice about it. Expressing my feelings of disappointment to this doctor made me feel more in control regarding my healing process.

After this horrible fiasco it was time for my first appointment with the healer, Gary Elder. I looked forward to finally meeting him. My therapist had told me he was well known in Europe, an American living in Italy. He worked on both continents giving seminars in healing and therapeutic touch to nurses and people interested in tapping into their own healing abilities.

Gary Elder was a tall dark haired man in his mid thirties.

He looked in good physical condition, not too fat, not too thin. He worked in a similar way to my previous healer, placing his hands around the face, and forehead, then moving to my shoulders which always held a great deal of tension. With the other healer the energy in my body would seem to shift, even though I was healthy. Now having a disease that required attention made quite a difference. I needed a healer who could really heal me, heal the aches and pains that now invaded my body. My first visit brought no lessening of my discomfort. The pain remained, but being relieved the pains weren't worse, thought it only fair to give him another chance. Most healers do not promise a cure, and having a serious disease, no miracles were expected. Although not expecting to feel much better after the first session, it would have been nice if there were even a slight difference. He had a good reputation so I was willing to give him the benefit of the doubt. Also, there was no other healer to try so we set up another appointment. My disease might be too much for even the best of healers anyway.

At my next appointment we discussed the changes in my dental work. Gary Elder was interested and thought that possibly the various metals used in jewelry making may have also influenced my condition. I mentioned the dry cleaner that sat directly under my apartment. He replied that the disease could have been in response to my environment and would look into it. He never brought it up again.

The cold had invaded my body. I used to love the cold weather and especially the snow. Now the cold was painful. Even in fifty-degree weather, gloves became a necessity. The colder it became the more gloves I wore, placing one pair on top of another. It was the same with my feet, the need to layer my socks. Gary told me to wear cashmere to keep warm. He said this was the warmest material. It had something to do with the electricity in cashmere. I had never worn any wool, always feeling too warm and itchy and only wore cotton. Gary said I should definitely wear cashmere gloves even if I didn't want to get a sweater. At our next appointment, he gave me a few pair of cashmere gloves brought back from Italy. I appreciated his thoughtfulness and immediately put them on. My fingers had become more difficult to straighten and if the material was too stiff my hands wouldn't go in, but these gloves were warm and soft enough for my fingers to slide magically into the finger holes. Now there was a new problem. My fingers were quickly wearing through the material, as if some invisible force of energy was burning from my finger tips, and making holes in the gloves. I joked that my energy was so hot it could burn right through the cashmere. Or was it my disease that quickly wasted away three pair of gloves? Gary was surprised by this reaction, but he wouldn't give up and continued to bring me gloves. He worked on me whenever he was in New York. After a few months he changed office space. Much to my surprise it was to the nutritionist's former office, right next to Dr. Elmaleh. "Small world," I thought. Unfortunately he wasn't making much difference in improving my health, so when he encouraged me to go to Italy and take healing classes with him, I bowed out. "Heal me first, then we will speak about your teaching me," was my thought. Our last discussion was about exorcism. I became concerned that he might try to explore that power on me and decided not to chance it. That terminated our relationship.

*I now longed for my old healer to appear. Let him come down from the clouds or wherever he had gone and stand before me. He had kept me strong, healthy. I believed if he were still near, none of this would have happened. No Scleroderma, nor pain to intrude on my sleep each night. I yearned for his healing touch, and hoped that someday soon he would return.*

There was a notice for a Scleroderma support group in a local paper. My husband suggested I call and relate my efforts in dealing with the disease, sharing my information with other people affected by Scleroderma. I agreed and spoke to the person in charge, relating the rapid progression of the disease in my body and how the many different therapies were now making a difference. I began by explaining the removal of my amalgam fillings, and their replacement with resin and holistic gold. She had heard nothing of this treatment in relation to autoimmune disease. She said she would make inquiries and wanted to know the cost. I continued by describing the difference diet had played in improving my health, particularly sacrificing dairy products. Her response surprised me. Giving up eating ice cream was not an option. A pint a night was her daily routine. She was not overweight. She was not interested in sorbet or any other substitutes. She was not willing to change her habits. I was not yet deterred and continued by telling her about vitamins and supplements. She responded by saying she took them once when she felt badly, but upon feeling better she stopped. While we spoke I told her my symptoms, how my skin hurt, plus my numerous aches and pains. She had experienced the same but resisted change. This was frustrating for me. Here was a description of symptoms that she herself felt, but after telling her how greatly I had been helped, it appeared to have made no impression. She had experienced many of the same pains. It is difficult for people to understand some of the sensations unless they have experienced them. She knew we had been through the same feelings. I couldn't understand how she wouldn't try some of the easy changes, even one as simple as giving up dairy. Just trying for a week would show a difference. When she responded that she would ask her doctor, it led me to believe she wouldn't try anything other than what he told her. I gave her my name and number so she could let me know about any meetings, but felt rather frustrated by her reaction, or rather non-reaction in not really wanting to change her habits. The phone call left me feeling confused, not understanding how someone would rather eat ice cream than feel better in terms of health. This attitude was completely contrary to my personal journey and beliefs. I refused to stop trying, refused to cease exploring every avenue towards good health and a full recovery. A laissez-faire attitude made no sense to me. Upon reflection, my feelings were a mixture of sadness and anger when our conversation was over. I couldn't understand how someone could hear my story and not be willing to try something different in order to feel better. It is one thing coming from someone who does not have the disease and cannot understand the pain and discomfort associated with Scleroderma. I was describing symptoms that she herself felt, and was telling her she could also improve her condition. It was frustrating for me, and left me wondering if there was a point of even trying to give people this information, considering this might be their reaction. Try something new. You might see a difference, and then you can decide to either continue in that direction or not. At least give it a chance.

She never called, not even about a meeting or anything else. I assumed she did not want to hear any more from me.

At about the time of my dental work, my mother heard a doctor speaking on a radio program. The topic was live cell therapy, particularly the effect of live thymus cells. She thought this might he be helpful. She called and told the doctor about my condition. He suggested I call and make an appointment. His office was in Manhattan so it was not a problem to get to see him. When we spoke on the telephone he told me about autoimmune disease in general. This doctor said that he had spoken to other doctors about 20 years ago who had patients with autoimmune diseases. At that time the doctors thought the right treatment would be to suppress the immune system with cortisone or prednisone and to be careful not to give any herbs or any nutrients that might cause an overreaction to the immune system. When he looked for literature or for scientific research, there was very little information. He began to realize what would happen if you took that immune system and stabilized it; whether or not it was overactive, under active or just not functioning properly because of some signaling mechanism. Basically that's what an autoimmune disease is, an over response of immune cells to break down a specific type of protein that plays a role in a connective tissue production. He also said that he had recently been speaking at a forum with a doctor from Arizona who had been having success in treating Scleroderma with thymus cells. There are a few different cell therapies for different diseases but the doctor in Arizona specialized in Scleroderma and had a treatment routine set up. I made an appointment with the doctor in New York. When we met, he had spoken to the Arizona doctor and had retained his therapy program. I asked for this other doctor's name, wanting to speak to him directly. He would not tell me who he was or exactly where he was located. I was suspicious about his secrecy but let this pass, wanting to try this therapy regimen.

The live thymus cells came to me directly from the lab, in vials of frozen liquid cells. The cells are from a bovine source, which is a live cell protein and uses extract from the thymus. The product is a dietary supplement derived from juvenile, farm-grown cows. It contains thymus proteins and peptides preserved frozen in their native form. This is processed bovine thymus gland (never synthesized). It came in seven-cubic centimeter vials. I had to defrost the vial and hold half of it under my tongue for five minutes. It had the taste and consistency of beef broth. Having always liked the taste of meat, and not having eaten any in a while brought back good memories. I had consumed a lot of worse tasting supplements in my search. This was very mild in comparison to most of them. It wasn't exactly the best taste first thing in the morning but I could deal with it. Then the other half went under my tongue for another five minutes. This procedure started with a vial every other day and then every week or two progressively lengthening the time between doses. The doctor charged five hundred dollars for a box of ten vials. It was expensive, but I believed it was worth a try. Within a few weeks I noticed that my skin was less shiny and also becoming softer. I spoke to Dr. Gaynor to inform him of my progress. He believed the dental work was more responsible for my progress than the live cell therapy. I agreed, but felt the thymus had helped my skin, believing it was most certainly the combination of diet, vitamins, meditation, dental work, and live cell therapy that resulted in halting the deterioration of my health and allowing my body to move closer to normalcy. I was pleased.

A few months later an incident occurred that surprised and upset me. It concerned the doctor who gave me the thymus cells. A lady from the Scleroderma Research Library and I had become friends. We discussed my various therapies, always emphasizing the importance of proper dental work. One day she called me on the phone to tell me about an article she had read in a publication devoted to health and alternative therapies. She came across an article written by the doctor with whom I had done the live cell therapy. He wrote about one of his patients using a pseudonym for her...June Parsons, a lonely, tense librarian living in New Jersey. She sounded suspiciously like me, in her attempts at treatment anyway. If he was going to use a false name, at least make it totally different. I had specifically asked him if he had any other Scleroderma patients. At the time his answer was no. The article angered me because he wanted the reader to believe that the patient (June) had tried many therapies including removal of her amalgam fillings, but nothing had worked. He went on about how diet and vitamins had not really worked and took all the credit for any change in her condition. He ended the article by writing that after taking the live thymus cells she had almost returned to normal. I felt it was outrageous that such a disservice could be printed. This doctor was trying to take all the credit for helping to control Scleroderma and would be taking advantage of anyone who contacted him to start this therapy. He was giving wrong information by saying the dental work didn't make any difference. That made the most difference in my condition of any of the treatments.

I couldn't let him get away with this, because it was incorrect information and besides I didn't like being pegged as a lonely, tense, librarian. I called, pretending never to have read the article. "Give a person enough rope, and he will hang himself."

We had a short repartee over the phone during which time he seemed somewhat uncomfortable. Then he mentioned his article. I told him that I was working on a book about Scleroderma. Would it be possible for me to speak with this other patient, this June Parsons, to compare notes? He became evasive saying she would not want to speak with me, but that he would talk to her and call me back. No surprise when I never heard from him. This entire incident angered me very much. By his writing an article saying that the live cell was the only thing that worked, he was giving the wrong impression about how one should treat this disease. You have to try many different therapies in order to find the combination that works best for you. Doing one thing alone might help, but it is not the final solution. It was wrong of this doctor to make it appear that he had the only answer. It is very important to keep an open mind and get what information you can from each doctor that you consult. Unfortunately there is no one miracle cure and one has to be careful of any doctor who claims to have all the answers.

I wanted to continue using the live thymus cell and was lucky enough to find a naturopathic doctor who was able to order them for me. After relaying my experience with the other doctor, she was saddened, and believed that at times a doctor's ego can interfere with helping others. To add insult to injury I discovered the actual cost of the vials was a third of what I had previously paid. My new doctor was more interested in the healing process than the money and gave me direct contact with the lab to obtain the live cells.

I continued to take a vial once every four to six weeks, but when the box was finished stopped the live cell therapy, believing I had gone as far as possible with this treatment. I kept in touch with this naturopath, and used her to treat my son's allergies. She was honestly trying to help people, unlike the other doctor who was more interested in money and writing articles for his ego. Sometimes it can be disappointing and one can get disillusioned. You want to think that alternative practitioners might be a little more ethical in their desire to help people, but this is not always the case. My suggestion is to keep an open mind and continue doing research in finding doctors and practitioners who you can trust.

My basic routine stayed the same since experiencing a positive change in my body. I had been going for physical therapy. There were three different therapists who worked mainly on my hands, mostly by stretching my fingers and working up to my shoulders. They started with heat and then worked on the joints and muscles, showing me finger exercises to do at home. I was never very good at doing any exercise by myself and didn't do too much between appointments. One therapist even used electric currents while my hands were submerged in a basin of water. This physical therapy didn't seem to be doing much good. It was covered by my insurance but if I was going to take my time and energy, it needed to be on something that would make a difference. By this time my hands were very swollen and painful, and couldn't straighten out or make a fist. These therapists tried to keep some sort of movement in my fingers. Even though my hands were bothering me more than any other part of me, my entire body was involved. My skin tone was fairly good but an overall treatment was needed, not just on my hands. I asked the guided imagery therapist if she knew a good physical therapist. She suggested a woman she knew who was working with Scleroderma patients.

Frania Zins is a physical therapist using the Feldenkrais method. This therapy is a form of preventive medicine. It teaches you how to move without causing damage to the body. This is done through a series of gentle manipulations; the mind learns as well as the body. The two become inseparable, since every manipulation is specifically designed to send a message to the brain. The aim is to re-program the brain, not muscle building and strength through repetition. By moving different parts of your body, gently and subtly, those parts of your body can find new possibilities, until the entire body functions better as a whole. The emphasis is not on what you do, but how you perform a movement. Since everything is connected it makes sense to work the whole body and not just the spots that are most affected. This technique was helpful because it worked every part of me, but even with showing me new ways to do everyday things to take some of the pressure off of my hands, my hands still remained stiff and weak. I could not even grasp a door handle because my hands wouldn't close around the knob. It also became difficult to keep my grip and twist my wrist to open a door. Several occasions of becoming trapped in the bathroom taught me to leave the door slightly ajar, making it easy to push open and get out. It was becoming more and more frustrating. I couldn't do any of the jewelry work that had been my life, I was in pain and totally uncomfortable, and now couldn't even get out of the bathroom!!

Thinking that by doing everything else, my entire body would naturally heal, I had neglected my finger exercises, which the original physical therapists had showed me. This mistake became apparent when three of the fingers on my right hand began contracting. The realization came too late as to the importance of the exercises for my hands as well as general range of motion movements for my entire body.

Frania showed me new ways to do everyday movements to relieve some of the pressure from my hands. There were many things I did during a normal day and always took for granted. Most of each day was spent driving my son to school downtown and picking him up. Most of my errands were now done in the car, driving all over the city. Staying on the West Side, I was usually able to find a parking meter, and ended up spending a lot of time in the car. There were times both hands were needed to turn the key in the ignition, but my biggest problem was pulling the shoulder seat belt down and across. Frania showed me a way to accomplish this. She had me turn my upper torso to the left, grasp the belt with my right hand and then bring the belt down across my body to clip it shut.

After owning the same car for eleven years, it was time to trade it in. Looking for a new car brought along a new set of problems not previously thought about. I was used to stepping up into my SUV, but when we tried out a sedan or station wagon, I would fall into the car, which was lower than my standing position. Upon trying to get out I discovered I was stuck, and didn't have enough arm strength to pull myself up by the door handle, or the leg strength to push myself up and out of the car.

We finally decided upon a Jeep which was high enough to step into and easy enough for exiting. Frania's helpful suggestions helped to relieve the daily pressures of driving.

In the fall of 1996 we decided to move out of New York City. Westchester was our first choice, because of its close proximity to Manhattan where my husband worked and where all of my doctors were located. We also wanted to place my son in a good school district and decided on an area. I was very specific in my needs and did not want any stairs on the outside of the house. Though my overall condition had improved, the greatest challenge was the cold. Luckily winter had not yet arrived when we began house hunting, but as the weeks went by it got colder. My hands and feet immediately felt frozen. Any temperature below 50 degrees bothered me. I could move my legs easily in the warmth but now both my legs and ankles had stiffened, and upon entering a house I had to pause between each step. It was taking me longer to use even the steps inside. The thought of having to do it outside where it was cold was unbearable. I was afraid if my condition actually got much worse I wouldn't be able to walk around in the cold at all much less walk a flight of stairs outside. Though believing that all my therapies and dental work had made a huge difference, there was a faint voice in the back of my head saying, "What if the Scleroderma still isn't under control?" I knew it was important to protect myself if the disease began to move in the wrong direction. I didn't think it would but I wanted to be prepared for any developments, whether positive or negative. This didn't make it easy for our real estate agent. Westchester can be very hilly, especially the area we were looking in. The agent tried to get me to look at a variety of houses. I was definite in not wanting to look at anything with outside steps, feeling the cold just looking at them. Stairs inside the house would work. Even if it took an hour to go up a flight of stairs, at least it would be inside where it was warm. Eventually we did find a place that suited our needs. It was already spring and the weather was becoming warmer. There was a flight of stairs inside the house, but only two steps outside to the front door. We finally moved into our new house in July 1997.

Once imbedded in Westchester it became difficult to drive to Manhattan to see Frania. I had to go while my son was in school and there was always a lot of traffic. The drive turned into an endless three hour round trip. Aside from the time involved it would get very uncomfortable sitting for such a long time. This caused my hands to ache from holding the steering wheel. It also placed a strain on my back and legs. Frania had helped me, but the amount of driving was no longer possible, and I asked her to recommend someone in Westchester. Since she was so well acquainted with my condition, I asked if she knew someone who would be able to help me and who would be closer to my home. She knew me well enough by then to know that I was very selective about whom I actually would trust. Frania recommended a truly wonderful physical therapist.

Deborah Gerard was her name and Frania said she had "golden hands." She lived on the other side of Westchester, but it was less than 30 minutes away, an easy drive after all the time I had spent going in and out of the city. I made an appointment to see her a few days later. Deborah's technique was a combination of Feldenkrais and Craniosacral therapy plus her intuitive feelings as to where to work. After our first session I was thrilled. As if by magic she knew exactly where all the aches were, easing the strain in each area and working the joints and muscles so they were as aligned and relaxed as possible. We got together once a week continuously from then on. By working around my body, Deborah was able to get everything moving the way it was supposed to. The few times

I had to cancel an appointment, my body really felt it. I had complete confidence in her doing only what was in my best interest, knowing she would always do the right thing and not hurt me. Feeling very relieved in finding someone who could help me feel physically better, let me relax emotionally as well and trust what she was also doing for my mental state. I was very lucky to find Deborah. Frania was right when she said Deborah had "golden hands".

With constant work being done on my body, it was surprising to find the fingers of my right hand becoming more bent. There was an infection on my little finger caused by the bone pressing against the skin. It hurt constantly. The knuckle became red, painful, and my finger contracted further with every passing day, not letting me straighten my finger out to relieve the pressure. It was unbelievable that after having lived through so much, my right hand was now being hit, and hit hard. Of course, I was right handed. My jewelry career had stopped a while ago because of my hands. Now my lifestyle was further limited because my right hand was in even more pain. The ongoing frustration of feeling constant pain resulted in a loss of patience plus annoyance at having no control over the situation. I hated feeling this way and tried to stay optimistic but it was becoming more difficult. The sore on my finger had opened and was either oozing or bleeding. Thanksgiving was coming and we had invited 20 relatives over for dinner. I had always enjoyed the cooking and entertaining, but this year my outlook was a lot different. A prepared turkey was ordered and everyone was asked to bring a dish. It was not the way I liked to do things. All of my guests were glad to help, but I was not a happy girl, given all my limitations.

My check ups continued with Dr. Horowitz once a month. He prescribed antibiotics for my finger. Nothing helped. After two months with no relief, I was ready to cut my finger open and straighten it out myself. There seemed no other way of dealing with this problem. I couldn't take the pressure off my knuckle, and had no movement in that joint. Dr. Horowitz suggested calling Dr. Charles Melone. Dr. Melone is regarded as the most experienced and top hand surgeon for Scleroderma in the United States. In addition to his busy practice and teaching responsibilities, Dr. Melone has actively participated in both local and national programs of the United Scleroderma Foundation. His assistant was very nice and tried to fit me in but there were no cancellations so I had to wait a few weeks for my appointment.

**JANUARY 1998:** Dr. Melone has a very busy practice. I sat in the waiting room for three hours before being ushered in to his office. I immediately liked him and felt it was worth all the time spent sitting there. He spent a good amount of time speaking with me. During our time together he showed me before and after pictures of Scleroderma patients who had gone through surgery. Some appeared worse than me, but it was easy to identify with all the bent fingers. What I couldn't identify with, were the nail polished and manicured fingernails that called for attention. Why would anybody want people to notice their bent fingers? The answer to that question alluded me.

Dr. Melone explained how the contracted joints become progressively worse and there is a progressive ulceration of the fingers over the tops of those joints. What he made clear to me was by the fingers continuing to bend towards the palm of my hand, the open wound on my center knuckle keeps getting bigger. There only was an open sore on my little finger of my right hand, but the two fingers next to it were bending also. I knew from the experience on my pinky they would soon be severely bent and also have open wounds.

The doctor continued. He would straighten out my fingers and fuse the middle joint. When he fuses the center joint, he eradicates a joint that has already lost function. When he fuses the fingers, the bone grows across the joint and fuses into a more functional position. This also eradicates the infection. Dr. Melone said most doctors don't believe that a person with Scleroderma can heal effectively. He did not agree. He discussed other patients he had operated on and how they had healed very well after the surgery. He thought that by straightening the finger the circulation improved and this allowed the healing process to proceed. Dr. Melone believed that the patient should have options when dealing with serious hand problems due to the Scleroderma. A person can't just believe what one doctor tells them. I asked what other doctors might do in this situation. He replied that they would amputate the fingers.... Oh, really, now. I didn't think so. Not being ready to lose any body parts, an appointment was made immediately for the operation. My index finger still had movement though it didn't totally bend. I decided not to fuse the joint in that finger. It seemed that with movement in both the thumb and index finger it would be possible to use my right hand effectively. Even with three fingers fused, the important ones were the first two. My left hand was slightly bent and couldn't completely close, but it was nowhere near the contraction in my right hand. Dr. Melone thought we should watch it. I didn't want surgery on the other hand unless it was absolutely necessary. It was bad enough having one fused hand. Even though Dr. Melone said it would be useful after surgery, I wanted at least one original hand.

We had been planning to go away over my son's February school vacation. I asked Dr. Melone if the extra month would make any difference, knowing I would be out of commission for at least 8 weeks. We wanted to get in a vacation before dealing with the surgery and subsequent physical therapy. He said the extra couple of weeks would not matter.

The surgery was scheduled for the beginning of March. I called Dr. Elmaleh and she suggested homeopathic remedies to help me before the operation and then for the healing process afterwards. She had me take Arnica along with a few other remedies, some before and others after the procedure. I wanted to be in the best condition going into surgery.

The operation was performed on a Thursday afternoon. Dr. Melone scheduled these hand procedures as his last of the day. That way he could take all the time he needed to do this delicate surgery. It is very precise work and usually takes about one hour of actual surgery, but an overnight stay in the hospital was necessary. A regional anesthesia was used to numb my arm, although I would still be unconscious due to the anesthetic. The anesthesiologist was told of my fears. A bad experience had occurred during the birth of my son. I had been given too large a dose of anesthesia and felt the need to actively control my lungs, consciously breathing the air in and consciously exhaling. Trying to see if this was just in my head, I tried not concentrating on breathing, and didn't breathe at all. I had to keep focused on my life. I relayed this story to make it very clear that awakening in the middle of surgery and being put back under was preferable to never waking up at all. The anesthesiologist listened to my entire story. I felt that he did hear my fear about too high a dose of anesthesia. As it happened, I did wake up during the procedure. In my half drugged state came the realization I was still in the operating room with a doctor standing over me. Dr. Melone identified himself underneath his gown, cap, mask and glasses that had extra magnifiers sticking out. I couldn't see his face but the "Hi, It's me, Dr. Melone" was reassurance that I was in safe hands. He said not to worry, he was just finishing up and I fell back to sleep. Upon awakening, my hand and forearm were in a cast. I had some discomfort and was given pills to ease the pain. That night was spent in the hospital. It was not the most restful night due to the pain and also another person sharing the room with me and calling for help all night. Ah well, a good night's sleep was rarely in the picture any way.

At seven A.M. the next morning, I was pleasantly surprised to see Dr. Horowitz show up at my door. He wanted to know how I was feeling before going to his office. Always feeling Dr. Horowitz was a concerned and caring doctor, this visit made me even more certain about him being the best. An hour later someone from Dr. Melone's office came in to remove my cast and replace it with a new one. My hand looked scary. It was red and swollen with long metal pins sticking out of my three fingers. Dr. Melone's assistant changed the dressing and rewrapped my hand. I was sent home with my hand and arm tightly padded in a large foam "couch" to protect my hand, and make sure my arm remained in an upright position. It was uncomfortable, but I took the pills for pain and adjusted to sitting with my arm held in the air. My greatest difficulty was sleeping at night. My position in bed had to be lying on my back with my arm propped up. This did not allow for comfort and falling asleep was never easy, but I had no choice.

My follow up appointment with Dr. Melone was the following Tuesday. I always tried to get the first appointment of the day. Most doctors tend to get behind schedule as the day goes on. Dr. Melone could easily be behind by hours very quickly. It's always nice when a doctor spends time talking with you, unless you are the next patient waiting. The bandages were removed, than the doctor inspected my hand. It looked like something from a Frankenstein movie, with deep cut marks across my knuckles, which were clearly stitched together. There were four metal pins sticking out of each of my fingers above and below where the knuckles had been. It looked terrible but I tried not to despair. Dr. Melone said it looked really good and my hand was wrapped up again. Dr. Melone took X-rays of each finger at every appointment to better follow the healing process. Only when the bones had healed enough and entirely fused together would he remove the pins.

A week later I returned for a check up and change of bandage. The following week the cast was removed and a splint was made. The splint was a solid piece of plastic on the bottom of my hand and went part way up my forearm, then curled around my fingers for protection on the top. It was held together with straps that attached with Velcro. The splint was removed only to clean my hand, using alcohol to wash around the sutures and the pins in the morning and at night. Other then that my hand had to remain dry. This made it difficult to shower, having to wrap my hand in plastic to protect it from the water. Soon enough I was proficient with the use of one hand, my left hand at that. Of course I was right handed. I always wrote everything down, but now could barely read my own writing. It became almost impossible to cook, but I became quite good at making breakfast for my son Brian. He had always enjoyed pancakes in the morning. It was a challenge, which was soon mastered. Being able to dress myself became a new accomplishment. I bought a pair of shoes to slip on but didn't like them, and went back to my sneakers. It took perseverance, but I quickly got to the point where I could tie the shoelaces, and with only my left hand.

For me, the most difficult part of this experience was being unable to drive. Living in the suburbs entails spending a major part of each day in the car. During the week a friend graciously agreed to drive Brian to school everyday and pick him up at days end, but Brian was anxious about my condition so we all drove along for the drop off and pick up. On weekends my husband would do the driving, go to the supermarket, and run the usual errands. My mother always drove me into the City for my doctor's appointments. It would have been very difficult to survive under these circumstances if I didn't have the help and support of my family and friends.

This went on for another six weeks, all the while continuing my visits with Dr. Melone every two weeks. He was pleased that the healing was progressing so quickly. I told him about the vitamins and homeopathic preparations I was taking. He had no problems with any of it. I was happy that he seemed open to all of the alternative treatments.

When the splint and pins were finally removed, individual splints were placed on the three fingers that had undergone the surgery. These remained for another four weeks, but I was now able to drive and felt some amount of control returning to my life.

Dr. Melone next sent me to a hand therapist, Teri Weinstock. When he was deciding who to refer me to he asked where I lived. He wanted to suggest someone who was close to my home. It didn't matter to me where the office was located. If he thought it was the best therapy, I would travel anywhere. Teri worked on the other side of Westchester. It took me about 35 minutes to get to her office. She was well worth the time and driving involved. We worked twice a week and made great efforts with the exercises, pushing myself to get back as much movement as I could, as quickly as possible. Teri encouraged me to bend my hand from the joint at the base of my fingers. This became hard work having not moved my hand in over three months. Sweat poured down my face, but seemingly nothing was happening. Teri could see my efforts and gave moral support, but for me it felt like sheer frustration.

My follow up visits with Dr. Melone continued every week. He was very pleased with my progress, and considering my positive outlook on life, he believed I could go far with the aid of occupational therapy. Everyone offered much needed encouragement, spurring me on to make progress. As time past, little by little there was joint movement in my hand and also the top joint of my finger. Aside from the hard work, going to Teri's office was very enjoyable. She always had interesting people coming to work with her. She would boast about me to the other clients, telling them all the alternative therapies I had tried and how well they had worked. Suddenly I found myself speaking to the other people in her office on the importance of food and vitamins and having the right dental work. Teri tried to talk me into giving lectures, but that didn't interest me. My feeling was that most people didn't really want to help themselves. It was usually frustrating to even try to give advice. She thought I had so much good information that the least I could do was write it down. In that way people who wanted to know of my search for good health would have access to it. This idea intrigued me, so I began collecting information on Scleroderma and my various therapies.

I continued seeing Deborah Gerard to work on my body, knowing that she was the best physical therapist around. Aside from feeling much better after she worked on me, we had become very friendly. Both my body and my mind were benefiting from the time spent with Deborah. When she worked on me it made a tremendous difference in the way my body felt. When my hand was in the cast and I was not able to drive to see her, it worried me. I was very relieved and appreciative when she started coming to my house, carrying her massage table with her. Because I could not use my right hand, I began compensating with my left side. Using these different muscles, combined with all my stress made my body more uncomfortable than usual. Working with Deborah made me feel much better. Teri still worked on my hands, although less frequently. Teri tried to get the insurance company to extend the amount of visits they would allow me. The work she was doing with me continued to make a big difference in my hand movement. The insurance company refused. Not being able to afford the extra expense of covering Teri myself put an end to our sessions, but we stayed in touch. I now worked the exercises on my own to make sure to keep maximum movement in my hands. Deborah remained a constant in my life. There were a lot more aches and pains if much more than a week went by without seeing her.

After the operation, I believed the hardest part of my physical healing was over. The end was in sight. A week before the splint was to be removed there was an ad for a television show featuring my old healer Martin Obel. When my strange symptoms first started appearing, I had called his old number but he wasn't there. I tried to locate him but couldn't find him or anyone who knew his whereabouts. I had prayed for his return and lo and behold he was back. It felt as if fate had intervened to have him once again in my life, particularly at this time.

I watched the program and noticed his wife wearing one of my necklaces. I thought this to be a good sign. They were on television to promote the latest book he had written. I phoned the station and was given the telephone number of Martin's publisher. The following morning I called leaving my name and number, along with a small message. His wife, Elaine returned my call the next day. She asked if it was really me. My phone number was different than they had remembered, but they had hoped it was the same Jane Parker and called right away. She said they had been talking about me while preparing to tape the show, hoping I would see the interview and notice she was wearing my necklace.

"Of course I saw the interview, and the necklace was the first thing I noticed."

I then continued to tell her all my health problems, still believing Martin had returned at the right time to totally rid me of the Scleroderma. They had been flooded with calls after his TV interview, it helped that I had known them for 20 years. She gave me an appointment for the following weekend. Martin's own health had been giving him problems. They had moved to Europe so he could heal himself and had remained there for two years. During that time they completed the book that was now being released. Martin was just beginning to work on healing people again.

On my first visit with Martin, he had me lay flat on a massage table. He then placed his hands over my eyes and forehead. I could feel an intense heat flow from his hands and enter my body. There was also a vibration in his hands, although his hands remained still. Through this process I felt a moving and shifting in my being. He also had his own mental exercises to help the healing along. They were similar to the meditation and guided imagery I was already doing. I considered Martin a friend and told him about my many therapies, including the dental work. Much to my surprise he said that both he and his wife had dental problems, admitting it was bad enough to cause an infection in his mouth. He was taking a strong antibiotic to fight this condition. My heart sank. How could this be that Martin the great healer with a waiting room filled with people longing for his magic touch wasn't taking care of himself. I, the patient convinced him to see Dr. Gershon. Both he and his wife went. Martin had the first appointment. His mouth was so infected that by just touching a tooth, Dr. Gershon realized how inflamed his mouth had become. Both Martin and his wife blamed Dr. Gershon for hurting them. The dentist later assured me he had done nothing, and went on to say that Martin wouldn't even allow a cleaning much less actual work. I apologized to Dr. Gershon for sending him such difficult people. I did continue to see Martin, though finding it hard to believe he refused to address his dental problems. I

We worked together a few more times, but it didn't seem she was doing anything more than I could do myself. I stopped the Reiki work. Because Heidi was friendly with her, we would see her occasionally, but not in a professional capacity.

My dealing with what has affected me became an ongoing process. Though believing everything was under control, this did not hinder me from continuing my search for total reversal of my disease.

I believed I had run the gamut of both conventional and alternative healing. There seemed few options left, which made me wonder if there were any new roads to travel.

On my next visit with Dr. Horowitz he said the Scleroderma was not progressing and he was pleased, believing the disease was in remission and had been effectively stopped with all I had done. He thought it a positive sign that there were no side effects from the Penicillamine.

In the past Dr. Lieberman, the nutritionist, had said she suspected that the foremost reason I had not experienced side effects was because I was replacing all of the minerals being destroyed by the drug with vitamins. Because of this any negative effects were avoided while taking advantage of any good results that would occur from the medication.

I felt with the dental work, the help of my healers, the vitamins and supplements, my diet, the thymus therapy plus the physical therapy with Deborah, the Scleroderma would go into complete remission. It would disappear. This was my truth.

My next venture into healthy living was exercise. I had put it off being either too tired or having too many aches and stiff joints. Years before my illness I exercised all the time. Though never enjoying it, my body always felt better after a good work out. When a catalog from our local J.C.C. arrived, it contained an answer. Staring me in the face was a listing for an exercise class for women over forty or those who wanted to restart exercising. Since I fell into both categories, I signed up and was amused when I walked into my first session. I looked around to discover that everyone present was at least twenty years older then me. It appeared to be a class for senior citizens. The average age was approximately seventy-five. The teacher, a senior herself was in great shape. The class turned out to be fun and a great workout. It worked the entire body, using a combination of stretching, cardiovascular, plus light weight training. It was similar to the workout I used to do in the city but not as intense. Because it was for senior citizens, there were also a good amount of motion exercises, which was perfect for me. Most of these women had been exercising with this teacher for years. It was amazing what good shape these old birds were in. I became determined to get in as good condition as they were. They did exercises that were good for any age. Because my joints were affected I needed range of motion exercises that were not too strenuous. A program that dealt with older people had just the right kind of exercises to prevent me from hurting myself. Certain exercises were meant to counter osteoporosis. There were a series of flexibility movements in the hands and wrists. These were especially good because they gave me added movement where needed the most, in my hands. Having an exercise program that worked my entire body was very important. The cardiovascular and aerobics were also important to help open my breathing and circulation. All of the areas affected by the Scleroderma needed to be worked. The program made me feel much better both physically and mentally. I even enrolled my mother in the exercise class with me.

It was now the summer of 1999. I was feeling quite optimistic. The hand surgery was behind me and the physical therapy was going well. I had total confidence in Deborah and was also seeing Martin the healer regularly. But suddenly, in September, my father went into the hospital. He needed a valve replaced in his heart. We expected his stay to last only a few days, but something went terribly wrong. After the surgery my father was taken to intensive care where he was hooked to a respirator. The doctors kept him heavily sedated to prevent him from pulling out the hoses, tubes and wires that were attached to his face and body. Each day, after taking my son to school, I met my mother at the hospital, which was located in New Jersey. It was a long drive to reach a depressing destination. At first, my mother drove out and I met her there. Aside from the physical tiredness from all the driving, she was getting emotionally spent. The days turned into weeks and soon a whole month had disappeared. I no longer attended exercise class, needing the time to see my father. Both my mother and myself were quickly becoming exhausted. She started driving to my house and we would drive to the hospital together. I started worrying about her driving home herself and began picking her up at her house. My routine became; take my son to school, go pick up my mother and drive out to the hospital in New Jersey. We stayed with my father until I had to leave at around one o'clock to drive back to Westchester and pick up Brian after school. Many times my Mother would stay in the hospital with my father during my return trip to pick him up. I would bring Brian home, help him with his homework and prepare dinner. When my husband arrived home, I would make sure they ate, then drive back out to the hospital to pick up my mother, either taking her home or bringing her back to my house. I tried hard to keep my stress level under control, and knew it was important to make time to see Deborah. For me she became the one person keeping my body and head from falling apart.

I bought a healing tape with a subliminal message to bring a healthy reaction to the body, and brought a small tape recorder into my father's room. We kept the tape running during our entire visit. The only sound heard was that of soothing music. The nurses were both nice, and sympathetic, agreeing to keep rewinding the tape even in our absence. A few of the nurses liked the music so much, they would stop in my father's room to listen and relax. That made me happy. Not only were they nice to my mother and me, my father ended up getting extra attention.

There was no longer time to see Martin Obel. I made the time to see Deborah knowing she was helping, but felt a huge question mark when it came to Martin. The entire teeth episode concerned me. Though his powers may not be what they once were, I still had faith. Knowing that he used to visit patients in the hospital quite often, I asked if he would work on my father. I offered to pick him up, bring him to the hospital and drive him home. All the conversations took place through his wife. She did not want him to do it, and made it seem as if Martin was afraid that he might get ill if he went to a hospital. If that was true, he must have realized he was not at his full energy level, and if by chance he got sick he would not be able to heal himself. I finally was able to speak to Martin directly and asked him "Please, come help my father." He said no, but he volunteered to work over the telephone. He had never spoken of this method before, but it was the only way to get Martin's help. This required assistance from the nurses. There were no phones in the ICU and no cell phones were permitted in the hospital. I approached the friendliest nurse in the ward and broached the subject of healing through faith, having no idea if she was a religious person or only believed in conventional medicine. I didn't consider Martin's healing religious, but wanted to keep all lines of communication open when dealing with the nurse's unknown attitude towards healers. Continuing the conversation by saying there was a healer who could help my father, I went on to ask if she had faith in healing through prayer. Before waiting for an answer I asked if it was possible to arrange for a telephone in my father's room. Fortunately, it was the right nurse. Much to my surprise she had studied therapeutic touch and listened with interest to my unusual request. She agreed to let me borrow her nurse's telephone. These were the only cell phones permitted. It was a relief to be able to arrange for a phone that easily. As soon as the nurse handed me her phone, I called Martin to explain my father's condition, trying to be as exact as possible. He asked me to place the phone in my father's hand, and worked to send healing energy through the telephone wires. This lasted for thirty minutes. He asked me to call the following day to let him know my father's condition, but when I tried to reach him, again there was no getting past his wife. She hoped to appease me with a curt remark saying not to worry, Martin had been sending healthy thoughts to my father throughout the day. He did nothing more regarding my father. I felt disappointed, not believing that one session through the telephone could make much of a difference. I was right.

During this time, my mother went to the hospital every day. Aside from the one day a week working with Deborah, I was always with her. By now we both felt extremely tired from all the driving, plus the added strain of having to speak with the doctors and nurses every day. Unfortunately, stress was in the air. My mother was both worried and exhausted. I still had a few sessions coming to me with Martin Obel. These were appointments due me in exchange for the necklace given to his wife. I had seen Martin enough years when healthy to know he could help someone whose only problem was one of exhaustion. I called and once again was not allowed to speak with Martin, only to his wife. Explaining that my mother was not sick but did need a good shot of energy, her response was that Martin didn't see people who weren't sick. He had no time to give her. Her answer enraged me. Both Martin and his wife had known my parents for many years. Therefore, I did not believe this to be an unreasonable request.

After waiting a few days to sufficiently cool off, I telephoned Martin's office to make an appointment for myself, acting very nice and understanding of his refusal to treat my Mother. I was planning to use the time allotted me to tell him my thoughts, feeling that we had been friends for long enough that I could speak honestly to him.

Upon arriving at his office I was particularly careful not to say anything to his wife, but when Martin and I were finally left alone my feelings tumbled out of me. I expressed my disappointment at his refusal to see my mother particularly since she only needed to have her stamina re-enforced. His voice held a nostalgic note when recalling how he once did that for people, but it was now a thing of the past. I continued by saying I really was his friend and felt concerned for his health. His teeth were a mess plus he was always on one antibiotic or another. To work on people who had life threatening diseases was a total disservice. If he wouldn't do something about his own health, it was unfair he should work on people who really needed his help. I didn't think he was being honest with all the desperate people who traveled a long distance for an appointment.

At this point his wife burst into the room. She most certainly did not want me talking to him, and was worried about what I was saying, but it was my appointment and my twenty minutes to use as I pleased. Martin repeated my words to her. He sounded like a child tattle-tailing to his mother. She angrily told me I was taking up office time only to upset Martin. If there was a problem it should have been spoken about on the telephone. This was impossible, as I could never get through to him. She was angry that I told him he was taking advantage of people's desperation.

His wife closed the conversation by stating that if I wanted Martin to see my mother, I was free to make an appointment. A session of twenty minutes would cost seven hundred dollars. Yeah, right. I never went back. This entire experience was a major disappointment. As the saying goes…be careful what you wish for. I had expected so much more from Martin, and still wanted to take nothing away from his previous powers. When in his best form he could work wonders, but now he appeared to have squandered his gift by no longer taking his own health seriously. His priorities had certainly changed. He once helped others but now was wrapped up in his own publicity, and as a result he himself was no longer healthy.

Altogether my father was hospitalized for almost five months. He gradually came back to health, although he needed intense physical therapy to return to normal. The physical therapists at the rehabilitation center were amazed my Father progressed so quickly. Nothing keeps him down. He was always the most optimistic and determined person that I knew. He had been a pilot and navigator in the Air Force during WWII, flying 233 combat missions. The other men always wanted to fly with him, knowing "he always came back". This bravery and determination had always been a large part of his personality. As soon as he regained consciousness, he knew he would return to complete health. The first words he uttered were "I always came back." There would be no stopping him from achieving this goal. He had no doubts he would accomplish this return to his active lifestyle, and worked very hard for his reversal. He went home in February, was able to walk to the car, and then into his home. By the time the weather had become warmer, he was walking around very easily. Few people believed he would ever walk and lead an active life once again. He accomplished both of those goals. I am very grateful that both of my parents instilled in me a belief that I also could do anything I set my mind to. My personality reflects the determinism that was always present around my life.

During the months my Father was hospitalized, I put an extra five thousand miles on my car (not as many miles as my father covered during his flights in the war, but it had still added up) and became more focused on my parent's health than my own. I had gradually stopped the vitamins, feeling they were no longer working for me, and being too tired to count them all out and add the time on to my meals. I did continue the Penicillamine and my monthly visits with Dr. Horowitz, believing that as long as he continued to monitor me, I would be safe. During this time a major problem with the index finger on my right hand had been developing. This was the one finger that had not been fused during the first surgery. It was now very bent, and a round callous was forming, indicating the bone was pressing on the skin. By now I knew this was a sign of impending infection. Soon after the bone would start breaking through the skin.

Once again I sat in Dr. Melone's office. He believed surgery was the only solution and scheduled the operation in April 2000. Thank goodness it was only one finger this time instead of three. The surgery itself would take less time. It would be easier to get back to my usual lifestyle with only one splint on my hand. I was happy when the same anesthesiologist as I had for the first surgery walked in, and reminded him I would rather wake up during the procedure than not at all. The first time must have made an impression, since he remembered our original conversation. Once again, I started waking up while still in the operating room and felt very reassured when Dr. Melone greeted me. "Almost done" and I was back under.

As before, it was the same procedures after surgery, though this time everything was much easier. I was able to drive and continued to see Deborah. Teri was again in my life to work on my hands. My days were now taken up with various physical therapies. My schedule included three mornings a week working on myself.

Life moved smoothly, and by the summer I felt stronger, healthier, and decided once again to begin exercising. My friend Heidi recommended a personal trainer who gave a good overall work out. I set up a meeting and liked the sound of her program. She had me start on a treadmill, than moved to abdominal exercises. She wrapped ankle weights around my wrists since my hands couldn't grasp the dumbbells. It felt good exercising, so she encouraged me to do more. The first month was great. My body felt stronger which helped keep my spirits high. Then like a thunderbolt out of nowhere my muscles began aching. At first I thought it might be the exercise, but by October it became apparent to me it was more than that. My trainer felt terrible, believing she might have done something to hurt me. I reassured her it was not anyone's fault, knowing my own body well enough to know my limitations when it comes to exercise. These pains were coming from somewhere else entirely. The pains became so bad that every joint in my body hurt as never before. By my next visit with Dr. Horowitz a few days later, I could barely walk up and down the stairs in my house. Something was seriously wrong. The doctor watched me inch my way into his office. I gave him the bad news... the pain had now returned with a vengeance. He believed I was having a bad reaction to the Penicillamine, and told me to stop the medication immediately. He did not want to prescribe anything new until he saw the results of my blood tests. Dr. Horowitz called me as soon as he had the results. That was one of his traits that impressed me right from the start. His call came at ten o'clock at night. His diagnosis... My body was extremely inflamed. I suspected that by no longer taking the vitamins, all that the Penicillamine had been removing from my system had not been replaced. At that moment it made little difference how I managed to find myself in such a dire condition. It was too late to change what was already done.

Dr. Horowitz prescribed Prednisone to help the inflammation calm down, but even with the medicine the pain became a constant torture.

My legs were hit hard. I was used to pain in my upper body. This was a new set of problems. Going up and down stairs seemed to take forever. I moved one leg at a time, one step at a time, and then paused to recover. My legs felt heavy, as if they didn't belong to me. I had trouble bending each joint. My knees and my ankles stiffened. It took a good twenty minutes to navigate my way up the seven steps leading to the bedroom. Sleeping habits were turned upside down. When I finally undressed, and slipped gingerly into my nightgown, it was time to maneuver myself onto the bed, slowly lowering my body down, down, down, until reaching the mattress. The next step was to roll back onto the bed, helping my legs up with my arms. I began the night by lying on my back, but always moved around in my sleep. Now in whatever position my body settled. I was stuck. It hurt when my body tried to stretch out, and ached if I attempted to roll on my side or bend my legs. Once settled in a position with minimum pain I couldn't move. Any attempt to change my spot became an agony. There was no strength in my arms so I could not turn over. Sheer exhaustion finally allowed me to sleep, but any small movement awakened me with pain. Morning found me more tired than when I went to sleep. To get out of bed, I rolled to one side, allowing my legs to swing over the side of the bed, then proceeded to push myself up with my elbows to a sitting position. Next I had to stand and steady myself. This became my morning ritual, waking up at least 30 minutes earlier than usual. It took so much time to get out of bed. Then I first had to get dressed. This also took a lot longer than usual. Even bending over to put on my socks and shoes became an ordeal. I was in agony. Every movement became torture. I was in pain, and exhausted from not sleeping, but still kept to my daily routine. Each day I awakened my son, made breakfast and drove him to school.

The year before, feeling optimistic about my health, I began a business venture with Heidi. I had missed my artistic outlets and turned to photography. My limited hands were not much of a problem with a camera, just focus the lens and press a button, not many fine motor skills involved. In the past the pictures had been for my own pleasure. Now Heidi and I tried to turn this into a successful business. She enjoyed working in her garden, lovely flower beds surrounded her home. Our project began with pictures of her gardens and quickly developed into our own style of botanical photos. We produced a line of cards and journals that sold in shops around the country. Our business was installed in Heidi's house, with our office on the third floor. There was never any trouble running up and down the many staircases. Now it took me forever just to walk the few steps up to her front door. Out of necessity we moved our operation to the kitchen on the main floor. I felt badly watching Heidi run up and down the stairs with our supplies, but she could see my pain and insisted there was no better exercise than climbing stairs. We both knew it would take me forever to reach the third floor, and no work would get done if the time was spent hobbling around.

By November, my pains increased. Dr. Horowitz raised the Prednisone dosage because the blood work still showed a large amount of inflammation. I didn't need a test to tell me that. I was in agony. A high tolerance for pain had allowed me to live through great discomfort, but this was more than even I could bear.

Michael, my friend for twenty years, was also a confidant. Throughout my entire illness he had heard about all the aches and pains. Even after both hand surgeries I was still optimistic and going strong. He knew me better than anyone so when I used the word agony to describe my condition, he knew there was big trouble and he had to find someone to help me.

Within a few weeks, Michael called to say he found the real thing, a healer who could cure me. He sounded so certain, so sure that this healer, named Victor, would be my salvation. It surprised me. After my previous experience with healers, it would take no time at all to discover if he was the real thing. I trusted Michael's judgment and told him to make an appointment. After speaking to Victor, he called back to say that Victor was not interested in meeting new clients. He had told Michael he never heard of Scleroderma and was busy treating people with life threatening diseases. This left no time for him to see someone he thought had only a skin condition. Michael refused to take no for an answer, believing Victor was the right person to make me well. I knew if we were meant to get together, it would happen.

Victor and Michael had many conversations, mostly about health. Victor was very concerned about proper dental work. When Michael told him I had my entire mouth redone, this peaked Victor's interest. Michael went on to say that I would do whatever he asked regarding my health. He knew Victor held strong concerns when it came to wearing the proper clothing, sleeping on the right mattress, and underneath a specific quilt. I was willing to adhere to this regimen but not before meeting him. He finally agreed to meet me, probably to see if my dentist was any good. Victor had told Michael that no dentist could do the right job because they didn't know the right materials. He thought all my dental work would need to be redone. I was interested to see what Victor would say, being confident that all was right in my mouth.

I called and left a message, then waited a week but Victor did not return my call. I tried again. This time he was home, and apologized for not getting in touch with me, explaining he had mistakenly erased my number. An appointment was made for the following week. January 24th, 2001. A day that changed my life.

# Victor's Story

I WAS BORN AND GREW up in the U.S.S.R. Communist propaganda had a great influence on my intellectual development. My view was that of an atheist, none of us believed in God.

Everything was straightforward with no belief in religious truths. This took away many questions in the process of growing up. From the time I was young I liked to read science fiction books. This seemed more real than any miracles could provide.

After basic schooling, I did not want to continue my formal education, thinking the people who went to the institute (there were not colleges as in the United States) were not very bright. The institute gave instruction in your chosen profession, but I didn't have much faith in their teachings. Most people were just going so they could get a diploma. In the U.S.S.R. a diploma becomes a license to have a job. You do not have to work hard. You could sit on a chair all day and do almost nothing. The most important thing was to come on time in the morning and not check out early at night. You didn't have to be smart. In fact, you could even be stupid, but you would always have a job and earn money. It was almost impossible to be fired. If you had a diploma you could get a job and be paid by the Communistic System. The type of job you had would dictate how much money you could earn. Very often, a skilled worker could make more money than someone with a diploma, even the boss of the company. The young specialists in different fields of work all had diplomas but were clueless to what they were doing. This set me on the right path, because no one could explain the advantage of an education in the U.S.S.R. I had no respect for organized higher education. My friends were carefree and also weren't interested in continuing their education. If one of my friends decided to go on with his studies, we thought his life would be very sad because he couldn't go out and play. We had jokes about some of the people with diplomas being jealous of the workers without an education. We were making more money than they were. The type of people who went to the institute was the ones who didn't have sharp brains. In my opinion these people could not think logically. If I was one of them I couldn't respect myself, and would bring myself down to their intellectual level.

My intuition told me I had more knowledge than the people who went to the institute. All the technical terms that they learned didn't seem necessary to me. I was able to speak of many things without using technical terminology, and felt I had a higher level of understanding than they did.

I never thought about my future. As a teenager I learned how to fight. In my area, you needed to know how to defend yourself. I taught myself and usually won all the fights, but never went looking for trouble. Before using my fists I tried to find a way out of the situation. This helped me in my outlook on life, searching to find answers to many questions that seemingly have no answers. As a naïve teenager, I dreamed about what was written in my science fiction books. I wanted to find something that existed in life that was equal to those amazing stories.

The years after my formal schooling can be summed up easily. I was in the army, and after that got a job in Siberia working for companies that searched for oil. I tried doing different jobs, but they were all very simple to me. I loved Siberia. It had a big, beautiful countryside. It is not all ice, snow and desolation described by people who have never even been there. I was in love, but eventually separated from my common law wife. We had a daughter together, and when we decided to separate, I moved to Yalta. Yalta is considered the most beautiful location in the U.S.S.R.

At this time, Gorbachev came into office. With Perestroika people were finally allowed to start personal businesses. I found it easy to make money. If you were enterprising enough there were many opportunities. In the past this was not possible, even if you were smart. Now I created a variety of businesses which all made a profit. Video movie theaters were developing throughout all of Russia. The theaters were usually built around train stations, airports, and big business buildings. The price to go see a video was only one ruble, and you could watch an American movie. People who owned their own video equipment, along with small television sets, were buying videotapes with Russian translations and showing them. The popular actors were Stallone, Schwarzenegger, Eddie Murphy, Charles Bronson and other action heroes.

Many people came to Yalta on vacation, and if I opened one of these theaters, it would be easy for me to make money. I organized this plan, by bringing friends who already had the equipment and movies to my city. We split the money fifty-fifty. A small club was rented, sometimes used as a movie theatre, other times turned into a lecture hall. We put two twenty-one inch television sets in the front of the hall, and we always had a theater full of people. I made a lot of money and paid the cashier, the cleaning ladies, plus the people who gave out business permits. They were all paid well, which made them loyal. I went on to organize other theaters in another city on the beach. Everything I did made money.

One day in Moscow while looking for video equipment, I found a game that when punched, measured your strength. There was always a long line to play this machine. In fact I used it so much my fist hurt by the end of the evening. It seemed a good game for another business in Yalta, but it was difficult to locate the owner. People involved with this machine thought I was in a racket and looking for some kind of pay off. Finally, after much convincing they gave me the owner's phone number. He wanted four hundred rubles for the machine. I told him I would pay one thousand rubles if he could send the equipment to me within two weeks time. It arrived a month and a half later, but the money was made back in less than a week.

Later I organized diagnostic centers, finding the office space and getting the equipment. There were new technology computers that tested electrical points on your fingertips and on your legs. These computers analyzed the information and diagnosed the patient's health. Doctors were hired to work the equipment. They were happy to make the money. My friend told me, "Victor, all your money is coming from selling air." It was true.

Accidentally, I discovered I was able to heal people. In the past, I never believed in healers. I thought this belief was only for the uneducated, the superstitious, and the elderly from the villages, and was always skeptical. Only doctors and medicine had the answers to help sick people, no one could change my mind. While in my twenties mysterious stories were told to me about people being healers or psychics. The propaganda machine in the Soviet Union taught us that miracles did not exist. I had heard of certain herbs that helped people, but not healers and psychics definitely could not predict the future. To me the only miracles that existed were in children's stories. In one story there is life and death water that can put a person back together and bring him back from the dead. This was just a fairy tale. Only a child would believe in miracles. I felt the same about the stories told to me of healers, strongly denying everything about them. But you never know. One of my friends later joked saying, "It's very funny about Victor. For God to have given him the ability to heal people, it shows He must have a great sense of humor."

I don't want people to think my atheist views have changed, but after everything that has happened to me, it is hard to say with certainty that something doesn't exist. I still believe there has to be a rational explanation for anything that looks like a miracle. Through all my research I have been able to find reasonable explanations for many occurrences that were seemingly miracles.

There were times I met professors and had a chance to have scientific discussions with them. They had books with all the latest scientific discoveries and we would have conversations about one theory or another. The professors always said how impressed they were with my extraordinary thoughts. It was easy for me to explain how to invent different products. I spoke with a professor about a theory to create lasers for the army, explaining how easy it would be to actually produce these machines. He was interested and encouraged me to go to Moscow to study at the institute to become better educated. He believed it might be satisfying for me to do scientific research, and thought I might even make new scientific discoveries. He offered financial support for me to continue my studies. "The institute will make you more knowledgeable," he said. My answer came back quickly. "I don't want to go there. You can see I am smart enough to argue with you about your inventions. I have even given you a few new and interesting ideas, so what could the institute offer me?"

At that time, I was sure my knowledge was more than could be learned in school. Maybe this sounds arrogant, but to me the thoughts we had spoken about during our conversation all seemed obvious. For him to believe my thinking was so advanced without an education made me wonder what the institute could actually teach me. Again, this only confirmed my opinion of the people who continued schooling. Although my formal education was lacking, my knowledge was better than theirs. Even without knowing all the technical terms, it was easy for me to understand the theories behind them.

Using the correct terms was always my problem. In time, I tried to read books to educate myself, but stopped whenever there was scientific terminology and charts. The words made no difference. The thoughts behind the words were the important things.

There was another professor who was interested in my ideas. I brought a diagram of a perpetual motion machine I had drawn up and wanted to build to the Constructor's Bureau at the Research Institute. Everyone discouraged me, saying a perpetual motion machine is impossible to create. I showed them my diagram and explained how it worked. No one could argue with me. In fact, they became excited, and sent me to the head of the bureau. A scientist whose main interest was perpetual motion came to speak with me. He knew all the studies and inventions created in this field. With just a quick look at my drawing, he immediately denied it could work. But upon questioning, he could not explain why he thought it would fail. My explaining its possibilities was more persuasive than his belief in its failure. The professor told me to return in two days. They needed time to think about it. When I returned, he told me all the scientists had become very excited, even stopping their work to think about it. I asked him to just make one machine. It was very simple. Then they could see if it worked or not. This time he asked me to come back in one week. The week passed, and he asked me to give them another week to disprove it. The entire Bureau had become excited about my drawing. He was finally able to give me an explanation as to why it would not work. At the same time he invited me to come to his institute and do research. He showed interest in my thought process. Again, I declined, telling him, "Your whole bureau took a few weeks to find an answer for an uneducated guy. What could I learn here?"

At the time I had a friend who was going to a healing school. She told me, "Victor, you need to go to this healing school. You have a lot of power. You could be the best healer." I never thought about having powers. Having extra powers and super abilities didn't impress me. I believe we all come from the same material, why should anyone have more power than any other. I answered her, "Better you go to this school by yourself and don't bother me about it." I was busy developing new businesses and had no time for listening to her talk about healing. She never tried anything she learned in this school on me because she knew of my skepticism towards healers. She wanted to explain certain techniques, but I showed no interest.

One time in Moscow a reporter from a news channel was video taping a man on the street who claimed he was performing a healing. He moved his hands all around a woman's head. This was the first time I had seen anything like that. When the healer stopped, the journalist spoke to this woman, wanting to know how she felt. She said she felt the same. No better, no worse. It was not at all interesting. The healing techniques the man was using had not worked.

I had heard about a famous healer in the Soviet Union who was holding a mass healing and being curious, decided to go. I didn't think any real healing would take place. I went with a friend who brought a video camera, wanting to tape whatever might happen. My friend with the camera was not allowed in. This made me even more suspicious. Why wouldn't they allow someone to tape the healer? They must be afraid that some trick they were using would show up on the video. After staying for the complete session, nothing was different, but the next morning, I felt completely changed. It was as if I had just returned from a relaxing vacation. This session had a strong influence on me. I began to believe some of the stories people said of this healer, and how they had been helped. Many at the mass healing brought medical testimonies. Everything seemed legitimate. Maybe this healer actually was able to really help people.

After awhile, I met a girl who had studied at a healing school. She told me she was able to heal people. I had a slight headache at the time, and decided to test her. Recalling the man in the street trying to heal the woman for the television camera, I asked this girl if she waved her hands around while she did her healing. She said yes. I told her if she took away my headache I would arrange for her to get good office space to open a business. Having enough connections to place her in a good location, she had to show me she could do what she promised. In about fifteen minutes, my headache was gone. I called my friend and arranged to get her an office, which was close to mine. When she moved in I went to speak with her, asking her questions about healing and how it worked technically. She had no rational answers for me, and spoke of mysterious meditation and prayers. She said you must sit and pray, then ask forgiveness of all the people you may have hurt. This will be helpful to your soul and give you good health. I was very healthy without forgiveness and without praying and didn't believe this explanation. Then she tried to tell me about moving energy. None of this made sense to me. I continued to question her until she finally said, "Victor, I do nothing with these people who come to see me. I just tell them to pray. They become rested after sitting in a chair and praying for thirty minutes, which makes them feel better." This made me very upset. To me it looked as though she was cheating people. I told her, "You can't do this. Men and women, even children come to you for help, pay you money, you need to do your job." She smiled and shrugged her shoulders. "You could see that I have the power to heal because I did remove your headache but if I used my powers too often I would always be tired." I didn't like her answer. She received no more help from me after that.

Other healers came to her office. They spoke of auras and other strange things. I even met a man who claimed he could see a mile underground. I had to laugh, and told him, "If this is true you shouldn't stay here. Go to the oil companies with your wonderful powers." I had worked for an oil company for fifteen years searching for oil. If you can tell them where the oil is hiding they will pay you any amount of money. Maybe he could also see gold or diamonds, even other minerals. My skepticism only got stronger after listening to these people. They all seemed crazy. I never wanted to be like any of them. But life is full of surprises.

My own healing work started by accident, after going to the theatre with a friend. He told me he had a terrible headache. We went inside, and he sat down on the other side of the lobby. I liked to tease people and said to him, "I'm going to heal you." I held my arm up in his direction, with my hand facing him for just a few seconds, and then lowered my arm. After seeing other healers who seemed to be putting on an act, I felt I had played a pretty good joke. Then, a minute later he said "Victor, I don't have a headache anymore." I didn't really care whether his head hurt or not. He continued, "No Victor, it's never happened before. With a headache as bad as that, I always need to take a handful of pills. These headaches are horrible and never disappear right away. Even when I take medicine, it always takes at least two hours for me to feel better." I paid little attention to his words. My friend and myself now sat together near an older woman who worked as a cashier in the theatre. She had once worked for me.

She had seen everything that took place between me and my friend. She spoke. "Victor, I have a problem with my kidney. You need to hold my kidney. I know you will be able to heal me." I thought she must be crazy. If she was a young woman, it would have been enjoyable to look for her kidney, but did this older woman just want me to put my hand on her? I didn't even know where the kidneys were located. With all of my medical knowledge, kidneys and ovaries and other women's organs were all in the same place. In the Russian language, all the organs sound similar. I was very shy about working on her, but she was stubborn. She told me, "Victor, come hold my kidney." I asked innocently, "Where is the kidney?" I breathed a sigh of relief when she showed me an area on her back. She said the problem was in her right kidney. Moving closer, people started gathering to watch. I placed my hand on the area of her back where she said her kidney was, and felt nothing. I was afraid that people might wonder why I was holding the back of a much older woman. She said she felt a lot of heat, but continued to sell tickets the entire time I worked on her. I held my hand over her back for close to forty minutes.

The next time I went to the theatre, she told me her problem disappeared. Her doctor had said she would never be cured. I played it down, even laughed about it. Of course, when a younger man holds an older woman, all her problems disappear.

A week later, one of my friends came to visit complaining of a headache. I said, "Sit, I will treat you." For me, it was interesting, also funny. Was possible to repeat what I had done with my friend, or was it just a crazy incident? I held her head for about twenty minutes. This time there were no second thoughts. After all, I did know exactly where the head was located. After the twenty minutes had passed, she told me her headache had gone. She promised to bring her mother to see me, because she had suffered with headaches all her life. Three days later, she brought her mother to my home. Her mother said she took a handful of tablets every day to ease her pain. I held her head in my hands for almost four hours, until she told me her headache had disappeared. She no longer felt any discomfort. I ran into her one year later, and she wanted me to know that her headaches had never returned.

I was becoming more and more interested in the results I was having when I worked on people. Was my method only good for headaches or would it succeed with anything else? A few of my friends always complained of stomach problems. The first time I held my hand over this area, I was able to feel what was happening inside. I felt pulses signaling out from their stomachs, then a pain moved into my hand, but the sensation shifted. The tenseness in the stomach disappeared and became more relaxed. The quality of the circulation in the area improved. My hands no longer hurt. I knew a few people with the same problem and offered to work on them. They all felt better after seeing me.

I wasn't planning on being a healer. I just found it interesting to see what I could do for people, and was making enough money in my businesses so I did not need another job.

One day while taking the train to Moscow, I began a conversation with a couple in my compartment. The man said he was a famous artist, but he had a problem with his right arm. This had been developing over the past five years. His doctor's wanted to cut out a large portion of the muscle tissue. He did not want to have surgery because he was afraid he would lose the use of his arm. His arm was completely bandaged. I asked him to remove the bandage so I could see the problem. He agreed, showing me a large ulcer, a two-inch lump on his arm with liquid oozing out of a hole at the top. It was very red at the center, the rest was a dark blue black. After successfully treating ulcers inside the stomach, I felt there should be no problem altering any kind of ulcers that were outside the body. I told him I could change his condition. He looked skeptical, but his wife spoke to him, "Don't worry. You are not risking anything. Just let him try." I worked on the inflamed muscles in his arm away from the ulcer for five or six hours while riding on the train. As the inflammation went down I moved my hand closer and closer to the ulcer.

The first results showed up in less than an hour. His ulcer changed color and began shrinking. After about three hours it began to disappear. The liquid that had been present stopped oozing out of the ulcer. His skin was returning to an almost normal condition. He was amazed at my result. I didn't believe I was doing anything special, just making an effort and working hard to help him. He had been suffering for years. It had taken only a few hours to change the entire problem. He and his wife tried to convince me I had special powers. I didn't think so. Some unexplained force in me knew how to do it. The artist and his wife were very appreciative and wanted to give me a few of his paintings as thanks. He said his paintings were expensive outside of the country. He didn't need to give me anything. Dollars were of no value to me in Russia. I always helped people for no money. In my free time, I found it interesting to do this kind of work. Sometimes after working on people, I even gave them money. At this time in Russia, most people didn't have enough money for food. I did everything for my own research, not to make money.

There were two instances that really changed me, making my interest in healing grow stronger. My close friends knew about my skill. They also knew I wasn't really interested in being a healer. One day, my girlfriend and another one of our friends told me about a woman who had broken her back four months earlier. She suffered with great pain, and could hardly walk. They pleaded with me, "Victor, you need to heal her." I thought no one could fix this kind of problem. I never heard of anyone healing the spine. My friends kept insisting, repeating "you can do it." I was reluctant, but finally agreed to try.

We met at my girlfriend's house. She said I only had one hour to heal her friend because she had an important meeting to attend. I was curious to see what a broken spine actually looked like. I placed the palm of my hand about six to eight inches away from the area of her back where the break was, and began moving my hand up and down along the region of her spine. I felt a sharp scratching sensation in my palm from the area I had touched. It was as if a laser came from that spot and hit my hand. I found it very interesting that a laser signal was coming out of her back. I moved about six feet away still facing her back, and again felt the same sharp laser sensation when I held my palm towards her. I moved back another ten feet. The laser sensation was not as strong, but it was still there. It was as if her spine had a small hole in it. Energy was leaking out of this opening and acting like a laser. I asked my friend to put the palm of his hand behind the break area, wanting to test if I was imagining this sensation or if it was real. I wondered if he could feel the same thing I did. My friend agreed that he too felt a force coming from her back.

He had no powers but seemed to be sensitive to these things.

I wasn't sure of what to do, but reasoned that if I closed the leakage, she would have less pain and her spine would be able to work properly. That seemed only logical, if you were losing power through an area that was leaking, you would be weak. I had no idea how to close this hole, but decided to try, knowing it wouldn't hurt her. Based on my intuition, I started working. From across the room, I held up my palms towards her back. I began moving closer to her, all the while pushing my palm in her direction. I concentrated on returning the energy that was leaking out of her back. Trying very hard to keep the energy leakage in the center of my palm, I continued the pushing motion until I stood right behind her. Then I held my palm on her back over the leakage area. After awhile, I removed my hand, wanting to see if she still had leakage. I felt a small amount, but it was now in a slightly different direction. I placed my palm on the front of her body where the break was. There was also a small amount of leakage coming from there. I concentrated through my palm on closing this frontal leakage. After that, I felt no more leaks. Again I asked my friend to try and feel if the same leakage was still there, thinking I might have lost feeling in my hand from working so hard. He held up his hand and said he felt nothing. I asked the woman to stand up from the chair she was sitting on. She hadn't been able to bend down and touch her toes before I started. I asked her to try. She easily reached the floor and repeated this motion a few times. I then asked her to squat. She did this without pain. I asked her to twist her torso from side to side. She was able to accomplish this. That was that. It took about forty minutes. Her friends had told her, "Victor can heal you." She accepted that, and did not seem surprised that I made her well. I was the one who felt surprised. This surely was something very important happening to me. She called the next day to say she was doing anything she wanted without pain in her back. She asked when I would work on her again. I told her, "If you have no problem. Why do I need to work on you?" and I didn't.

Another time, one of my friends introduced me to his neighbor. This man's son suffered from Cerebral Palsy. He asked if I thought it would be possible to help the boy. It was by accident that we met, but it turned out to be important for my research and for both of us. When meeting his son, I understood the difficulty he had with small everyday movements, but even with his physical disabilities, the boy was unbelievably smart. He was almost seven years old and was starting school the next year. He could hardly walk, even with his parents support. His legs turned together at the knees and spread apart as they reached his feet. He did not have much control through his brain signals. He held his arms almost straight to his side. One arm was bent with the wrist turned down. He had trouble eating by himself because his arm and wrist would not bend enough to reach his mouth. It took tremendous effort to try bending his arm to his face. When he got near enough, he had difficulty putting the spoon into his mouth. He couldn't hold his hand straight up. His neck had no control through the muscles. Sergei's head hung down to the side as if there were no disc supports in his neck on that side. His head was hanging, his arms were barely working and his legs weren't moving properly, but he still seemed to be a very happy boy. He never complained. The doctors told his parents that Sergei would never improve. The family would have to learn to deal with it. The father worked for the Russian Army, which enabled him to see the best doctors in Russia. All these doctors said the same thing. There was no hope for improvement. I told Sergei, "We will make you better, you and me together." I was going to help him walk better and maybe change him totally. I started to work on him using the knowledge I had already uncovered. Every part of him had been damaged so I worked his entire body.

I felt there was not enough blood circulation, and because of this his bone marrow was not active. It didn't matter what was affected, his hands, his feet, his neck and spine were all connected to the bone marrow. I told his father the need to do intensive work on him, at least three to five days a week. His father told me he was going to a special school for children with cerebral palsy and because of Sergei's school schedule, we could only work one or two days a week. I didn't understand why the father would limit the time I worked on his son. With enough hours spent working on Sergei, he could get better. The father refused, causing me to feel extremely frustrated. The reality was that I could only work as much as the family allowed. My feeling was if I were the parent, I would do anything to help make my child healthy.

The first time I worked on Sergei, he became tired after two or three hours. He felt fatigued because through my work, his muscles were changing very quickly. His father stayed in the room with us to watch what I was doing. I told him there were exercises he could do with Sergei while I wasn't there that could help to improve his son's condition. He said, "Victor, I believe in you, but I'm not the specialist." I was surprised he did not want to help with the boy's healing process. Sergei had a younger brother who was about four years old. They fought a lot, and the younger brother was stronger, but they had a lot of love for each other. The brother always stayed in the room watching me work with Sergei. After a few times, the father no longer remained in the room, but the little brother continued to watch us. Sometimes he would get in the way and bother me asking what I was doing, particularly when I had to squeeze or twist Sergei's legs or arms. It was important to stretch the muscles to have a faster change in the body. After awhile the brother became bored and left the room. It was easier for me without the extra distractions.

I worked intensely on Sergei's neck. The doctors had told his family he had no muscles on one side. His neck would never be straight because there were no nerve connections. I didn't believe what they had said. After a few treatments something started changing in his neck. I could feel muscles developing in that area. The contraction on the other side of his neck began to relax. Little by little, his neck got straighter, and stopped hanging to one side. When he turned his head, it looked like he had more control of the movement. His wrist also began to strengthen and moved more naturally. It became easier for him to reach his mouth while eating. After a few months, he was even feeding himself without a problem because his arm was bending much better. Sergei saw the results, and told me he spoke to his physical therapist at school. He said I was going to make him walk normally and straighten his neck. Her response was unkind. "Sergei, no one can change you. You need to know you will be like this for the rest of your life." He was a smart boy with wisdom beyond his years, and told his physical therapist, "You will see how I will change." She did not believe him having never seen any major difference occur with this disease.

We worked for about five months, usually once a week, and at times every other week. When I was in Yalta there were no treatments for a few weeks at a time, but whenever in Moscow, I tried to see him. I still couldn't understand why his family refused to give me more time to work on him when I was there. His neck was now straight; almost completely normal after hanging down on one side. Even his walk had changed. That too was almost normal. Sergei's father told his parents about the improvement in his son's condition. They didn't want to listen, and think a healer could make their grandson so much better.

I was surprised when the father told me his own story. He admitted that two years earlier he only believed in conventional medicine. If anyone suggested alternative therapies he became very agitated, but he decided to do research. He read many books trying to gather information on cerebral palsy, but always found the same answer. "They tried to tell you it wasn't so bad. You could have a nice life. There was nothing to be done." After discovering that conventional medicine held no answers for him, he began his own search. This took him outside traditional medical knowledge. He read books about alternative therapies hoping for help in that direction. He consulted people who were supposed to be the best healers. The only thing they could do for him was to give hope. The father even went to school to learn how to be a healer, but he never tried anything he learned on his son. He said, "I didn't tell you any of this before. I was watching you carefully when you worked on Sergei. I knew nothing about you. You have no books published and aren't famous. You had no medical training and used no medical terminology. Yet you promised to heal my son." He believed my knowledge should be published, but I was not interested in publicity. I was just at the beginning of my research. Sergei was an important subject for me. It was frustrating to think the father had knowledge of alternative healing, but refused to help when I asked. After our talk, the father agreed to do certain exercises with his son. Two weeks later I returned to find Sergei much improved. Working with his father had helped, and Sergei continued to get better even while I was away.

There was a television show to raise money for children with cerebral palsy. Because of his previous condition and the fact that he was very smart, Sergei had been invited to appear on the show with his father. Because the father was successful, Sergei was always well dressed. At this time in Russia, most people did not have enough money to buy good clothes for their children. They often could not afford food. The father told me when they arrived at the television studio, no one understood why they were there. Sergei had no obvious signs of cerebral palsy. His walk was almost normal, and he was happy. The people in charge had not seen his previous condition. I was planning a trip to America, and though I didn't have a chance to completely heal him, I knew his life would be better than anyone could have imagined.

The most interesting story for me started in a taxi I was taking from Krasnogorsk. This is a town near Moscow where I was staying with a friend. The taxi driver told me a story about his daughter. She had recently had a baby and during childbirth, one of her hips became dislocated. Her leg and hip were swollen. She could hardly walk. The size of her hip was three or four times larger than normal. He had taken her to the best specialists, but no one had been able to help. She even went for special treatments at the Black Sea. I asked him, "Do you really love your daughter?" He said, "Yes. She, her husband and baby live in the apartment with us." I told him I could help her. I would go to their apartment and work on her if he would wait for me, then drive me back to Moscow. "Of course I will wait. If you help her, I will drive you anytime or anywhere without payment." Before we drove to his home, he wanted to know if I needed to make a stop to gather my instruments, thinking I might be a doctor. "No, my instruments are always with me. They are my hands." He said nothing, but I could tell he was curious.

When we arrived at his apartment, his daughter opened the door. She was about twenty four years old. She had a bad limp. It was easy to see that her left hip was much bigger than the right hip. Her father told her I was there to help. We sat in the bedroom, her father and mother sat across from us watching what I did. My work began on her leg by holding her ankle. I believed her condition was changeable. When I felt her circulation improving, I moved to her hip. At certain times I placed my hand on her back. It was taking many more hours than I originally thought. Eventually her father and mother left the room. After about three hours, the swelling in her hip had gone down. It was very interesting, because it smelled as if something was burning. When her hip was less swollen, I asked her if she needed to use the bathroom. The water that had made her hip so swollen had to go somewhere. She said she did not need the bathroom. I continued to work on her for another four and a half hours without stopping. Finally her hip looked and felt completely normal. I told her to stand up. She did. I told her to do a squat. She did seven of them. "Enough," I said. I asked her to move around and do different stretches. She had no problem with any of them. Her father was impressed and wanted to pay me. I told him, "I never charge people." He couldn't believe it, and wanted to give me something in return. He brought me two bottles of cognac. "Take – drink." Telling him I didn't drink, he insisted I take one bottle. I took it because my friend was a drinker, I would give it to him. Two days later, while leaving my friends house I heard someone screaming, "Victor, Victor." There was a stranger running in my direction. I didn't think this man was yelling for me. When he reached me he asked if I was Victor. I told him I was. "Then it must have been you who healed my wife two days ago. My father-in-law couldn't remember which entrance of the building you went in. We have spent the last two days trying to find you. My wife is doing very well, and I wanted to tell you I greatly appreciate what you did for her. Do you need to work on her some more?" I told him, no. I was quite sure the one session was enough. But even now, after many years, one thing still made an impression on me. Where did all the liquid go after the swelling went down in her hip? It looked to me as though she had at least a few gallons of liquid in there.

After that experience, my mind was completely changed. I became very interested in doing research. I wanted to find answers to change the problems affecting people's health. It was also very important to discover the cause of the problems. This curiosity pushed me to actively research different diseases. I wanted to succeed in all variety of healing. Until now, everything had come to me by accident. My friends knew about my healing ability, and would ask for help. If their problem sounded interesting I would work on them. My businesses were taking care of themselves. This gave me free time to work on my research.

My friend's wife brought me an illustrated book for nurses. She had bought it through a German publishing company. This book provided me with good explanations as to how the organs worked. I finally learned about all the parts of the body, realizing how much I instinctively understood and how well I had done without basic knowledge. This book made it easy for me to understand how the body worked without the need for formal training. The book supplied detailed pictures and explanations, making it simple for me to visualize where everything was located. I saw that my intuition had been right about many things. What I couldn't understand, was the fact that the book was successful in showing what was in the body and how everything was connected, but no one knew how to force these parts to work normally. I knew that many of the problems that

I read about were changeable, and believed these problems could be treated without the side affects of medication.

I decided it was time for me to leave for America. My friend had organized a few conferences about alternative healing methods. They were being held in New York and I was asked to be one of the speakers. I could not let this opportunity pass me by.

I was now living in New York with a Russian girlfriend. In Russia she was a successful marathon runner, but suddenly developed a problem with her immune system. I could not explain why, but I began working on her muscles. She was amazed at how fast she was now able to run in Central Park. As she got better, I felt my own health becoming worse. She knew that clothes and certain materials bothered me, so she bought me a sweatshirt with a hood and a pair of sweatpants. She knew what the most popular sports companies were, and felt they would have the best clothing. When I put them on and wore them for a while, I couldn't believe how good they felt. They were different from all the other clothes I had previously worn in the United States. It surprised me that she had actually found something that was comfortable. The only thing that bothered me was the tag in the neck of the sweatshirt. I cut the tag out, but this area continued to bother me. My girlfriend opened the seam, removing all the pieces of tag and threads that remained. After that the sweatshirt felt fine. There was only a small difference where the tag had once been.

## FREQUENCY

IS A NATURAL AND SUBLIMINAL VIBRATION, UNIQUE TO EACH AND EVERY DIFFERENT MATERIAL. A MATERIAL WITH HEALTH FREQUENCY FALLS WITHIN A SMALL RANGE OF AN ACCEPTABLE CENTRAL LEVEL OF FREQUENCY THAT IS COMPATIBLE WITH A HEALTHY

STATE OF BEING AND WILL NOT AFFECT THE BODY NEGATIVELY.

I understood that this tag held a strong frequency that recorded on this area. This bad frequency disappeared after a few months of wearing and laundering the shirt. Every time I didn't feel good I wore the sweatshirt and pants, sometimes even sleeping in them to feel better. I began searching for clothes that filled me with the same sense of well being as the sweatshirt. I went to many stores but had no luck finding any new pieces. My girlfriend told me she would buy me another good sweatshirt. She also bought me a jogging outfit. This time the new outfit was killing me, which made me realize she was just lucky the first time. I tried to wear these clothes, not wanting to hurt her feelings, but with each wearing, the effect on my body was becoming worse. The clothes made me feel tired. My muscles were not comfortable, as if the material was pulling energy from every muscle, especially in the neck area. Before wearing this outfit my muscles felt good, but the fabric took the natural, healthy feelings away. It was unexplainable, because the fabric was soft but my body hurt. I began to think that the company did not realize what they were producing, and without being aware of it, were destroying people's health, not helping them run faster. Even though I had my doubts, I continued wearing the bad outfit, but finally threw it away. I now understood how clothing could destroy people's health, and began my search for clothes from different companies. I eventually found cotton tank tops that were made from healthy material. Even the tags were good. It was gratifying to find the perfect shirt. I bought fifty of them, knowing at some point they would have to be replaced and afraid of not being able to find the same fabric. This had happened to me in the Soviet Union. Whenever I found something good and returned to buy more, it dismayed me to discover the item had been discontinued. I tried to remember what the proper material felt like so I could find the same thing somewhere else.

By now, I understood that the effect of the clothes was not psychological. It was definitely physical. My girlfriend had once been a top Russian marathon runner and knew what felt good on her body when she ran. She bought me a sweatshirt that made me feel healthy without knowing anything about the frequency of materials. She also bought me an outfit that had the reverse effect. It made me feel horrible. She eventually moved south, but we still talked. She agreed with my ideas about clothing, and remembered when she began running outside of Russia. She had bought herself a beautiful exercise outfit and wore it all the time because it looked good. But eventually she gave it away, finding it uncomfortable, and unable to use it for exercising. By then, I began to understand the importance of materials on the immune system. We both saw how the efficiency of her running depended on what she was wearing. This became a very important discovery for my work.

My friends, who had left Russia before me were now living in New York. They sent me clients because they believed in me and knew I could help people heal.

A man with skin problems came to see me. He had this condition his entire life. The only explanation his doctor could give him was that it might be genetic. He told me he was never able to walk barefoot. His skin hurt him so much, that at times he could not function. It was impossible to take a shower unless he used special creams. The best medical research specialists examined this man. No one could give him answers. There was no relief in sight. I felt quite sure I could help his condition, probably within a year's time. His skin was melted with a strong inflammation. It looked like psoriasis, but it was something different. As his treatments increased the inflammation lessened, but he complained that he felt no different. He said he would be happy if for just one day he would be without this inflammatory irritation in his body. On one occasion while walking down a flight of stairs together, he was forced to lean on the banister, groaning with every step he took because his feet were in such severe pain. I told him I could help, but he had to keep coming for his treatments. After a few months, he had days without pain or itching. Step by step the skin on his arms changed to a natural color, and his face no longer looked sunburned. He confessed that he liked to smoke marijuana on occasion. I believed it was slowing down his circulation. There were times he worried that he had symptoms of Multiple Sclerosis. I felt this was due to his smoking. He said the marijuana helped him forget his pain, and he felt more comfortable after he smoked. I knew exactly what the marijuana did. After he smoked, the inflammatory processes in his body increased. Each time, I had to waste hours of treatment cleaning his body from the influence of the marijuana. I did this by removing his unhealthy energy and replacing it with my own healthy frequency. This was done through my hands. Only after that could I begin working on his skin problems. Because of these set backs, the process of regeneration took much more time. We were working in opposite directions. I was cleaning his body, while he was provoking his body. It was very important for him to stop smoking. He promised he would, but didn't stop completely. The less he smoked, the more progress was made. There was also a bad influence coming from his teeth, which more than anything, affected his skin and his general health. Though he insisted he had a good dentist, I still did not like the work done in his mouth. I paid little attention to dental problems before, but with him I believed most of the inflammation in his body began with his teeth. I was working hard to change his condition but the changes came slower than I hoped. I once again spoke to him about his teeth, believing there had to be a dentist who could fix the problem. He refused to change dentists. It made it much harder for me to improve his health.

After more than a year his skin condition greatly improved. He even started running on a treadmill, and could shower without all his creams. I asked him to remove his shoes and socks and walk around the apartment. He did this without a problem, admitting he had never been able to do this before. Our relationship finally ended because he improved enough to be satisfied with his condition. Before departing I told him the importance of wearing clothes made from correct materials. I believed the business shirts and shoes he wore were damaging his skin and his health, but he refused to do anything about it. He said his shirts were made from pure cotton, each one costing a few hundred dollars. He could only work in clothes that looked good. I searched many stores for business shirts made from material beneficial to the health but found nothing.

As I met more and more people I noticed everyone had a smile full of American white teeth. There were no obvious gold teeth as in Russia. I soon discovered the importance of having the right dental work. After intense work on the telephone with a sick client, problems with her teeth began to bother me. This feeling became stronger and stronger.

I asked her if she had any pain or problems with her teeth. She said no, and believed she had a good dentist, but I knew something was wrong. There was no explanation, but the feelings from her teeth were going deeper into my teeth. Not fully realizing the impact of this, I continued to complain about her teeth, but eventually began to believe that it might be a problem with my own teeth.

I went to see a dentist. He told me I had a cavity, but there was too much pain to believe it was only that. He was a young dentist and probably needed money, because after finishing one filling he wanted to do another. I decided not to return.

My teeth problems continued. I knew I had to find answers. This forced me to begin my research, so I went to see a second Russian dentist. He listened to my theories, and agreed to give me various types of gold and porcelains for testing. I knew it was important to discover the differences. This was the first time a dentist had explained the various materials available for repairing teeth. Until then, I believed only metal affected the body. We never discussed the different porcelains or cements that could also be used. He showed me samples of white gold and yellow gold. When I tested the white gold, I didn't like the feel of it. I soon realized that many of these metals could cause blockages, which eventually might affect your entire health. Even the yellow gold was not completely good. I realized that the gold put in my teeth in Russia was almost perfect for the immune system. But this gold could not be put together with porcelain. The porcelain needs a much higher temperature than the gold they use in Russia. The dentist brought me different metals to try. Out of all of them, I chose only one gold, and even that one wasn't quite right. He made me a temporary bridge out of acrylic. Once more my teeth began to hurt. A day later, I was in excruciating pain. I called the dentist's office in need of immediate care. He wasn't at work that day, or the next day, or even the third day. No one could tell me why. He was likeable. He had helped me search for the right materials to use on my teeth. Now I was in terrible pain and couldn't find him. Where was he? A friend who knew this dentist looked at me in dismay while shaking his head.

His words surprised me. "Victor, he has a Russian problem. He's drinking. You won't see him for a week."

The pain was so strong, I felt my brain would be destroyed. I went to another dentist.

As my research continued, I realized that with most people their health problems began after having dental work. Now I understood the importance of that missing piece of information. There were times when I was not completely successful in healing people's physical health. I might be able to change it, but only temporarily because they returned years later with the same problems. Sometime the person's pain would manifest itself in a different part of the body. Knowing I had changed them, I couldn't understand why the condition returned. In the past I believed it was the clothing and bedding that created health problems. Now I felt convinced it was not only the materials we wore and slept on, but also the materials we used inside our teeth. With this new discovery, when I now worked on clients I tried to find out the kind of dental materials they had in their mouth. I asked about the cements, porcelains, and metals the dentist used. They asked their dentist and gave me the information I sought. Then I tried to analyze which one of my client's teeth felt the best. This information was filed away, to remind me of the names of the materials that were used. I quickly realized that the fault did not belong with the dentist. It was the different substances he put in your teeth that kept you healthy or made you sick.

A client living in California, called me on the telephone to ask about a problem concerning her grandson. He was five years old, and had chronic ear infections. He always complained about his bed, never wanting to sleep in it. He said when he slept in his parents bed he felt better. Both his mother and father believed his complaining was to attract attention, and be allowed to sleep in their bed. They always sent him back to his own room. Explaining to my friend that the wrong materials could make you sick, I suggested she sleep in his bed one night and then call me. She telephoned the next morning to say she had an ear infection just like her grandson. I had not told her this might happen. For me, it was an experiment. I wanted her to see for herself how materials could affect your health. She was impressed that I knew the cause of the problem and panicked about her grandson. What could she do to make him healthy? I told her to buy the quilts and sheets I recommended. Then she should use a few layers of quilts to make a mattress for him to sleep on. If she did this, I believed he would be fine. The first time she came to New York, she bought quilts and sheets for her entire family. When she returned to Los Angeles she made her grandson a mattress from the quilts. After that he had no more earaches. Of course, when you are healthy and powerful, bad materials can cause much stronger damage to your body than to people with weaker systems. These people have enough complaints concerning their health, and a few more do not make a big difference. This information is important for everyone. Most people don't realize where their problems are coming from. They go through many different medical procedures, take many medications, and complain to their therapists. Some people try using herbs, vitamins and natural products. All these remedies will not work without the right environment and the correct materials.

All health conditions are just mechanical. It has nothing to do with unexplainable or mysterious happenings. The knowledge I have gained through my research shows that all sicknesses come from some degree of mechanical damage to the cellular mass of the body. The body works like a computer. If you send a virus into a computer program, breaks form between the channels that command that program. The program will start to break down. The program becomes damaged. The same thing happens in the body. The person's genetic makeup and also their immune system have their own program. It has a very strong defense system. When people are ignorant about how to get healthy, or obtain correct information and choose not to follow it, they are able to break down even the strongest defenses. Through my research, I found damaging materials in a variety of products that people use every day. These necessary items break down the body's defense system and keep it from working to its full capacity. The medical knowledge that now exists tries to repair the damage to the immune system after it has collapsed. It can't be completely repaired because the problem continues to be triggered by the same environment that created it to begin with. The disease keeps coming back. It looks as if an answer will never be found as to how to successfully repair the body. In most cases, you can repair the damage you have already done. If you start changing to the right materials you will be able to reverse most of the damage.

Victor Dyment

# Working Together

VICTOR USUALLY TRAVELS TO HIS client's residence. Since I lived in Westchester, Michael suggested we meet in his Manhattan apartment. I was grateful for Michael's continued help and generosity.

I eagerly awaited my first meeting with Victor, thinking if nothing else, it would be interesting. I had faith in Michael, and when he said Victor was the real thing, I had to believe him. My optimism kicked into high gear at the thought of meeting the person who might be able to bring my health back. Before the day arrived I spoke to Deborah and Heidi, anticipating my appointment with Victor, the new healer. They expected this meeting to be no different than any of my other healer experiences. Having listened to my past stories, they looked forward to hearing about another absurd get together, which always produced laughter. I hoped this would be different.

In truth, I felt excited when the day finally arrived for the two of us to meet face to face. I tried to wear comfortable clothes, a black sweatshirt and a pair of cotton jersey pants with an elastic waist. Since my body was so inflamed, this was my daily outfit. The pants had been purchased at the time of my first hand surgery. I previously wore jeans all the time. When my hand was in a cast it was very difficult to work the snap and zipper on regular pants. I never liked pants that pulled on with elastic but quickly learned that with only the use of one hand they were much easier to live with. Now, with my entire body inflamed, I had pulled out these old pants and had been wearing them. I also slipped on the custom made low boots bought in New Mexico the year before. They were the most comfortable shoes I ever owned and I wore them constantly.

Never knowing what the traffic might be driving into Manhattan, I left early to give myself plenty of time. Victor had to be cajoled into seeing me, so it was important to be the first to arrive. I entered Michael's apartment fifteen minutes early. Victor came exactly on time. When I answered the door, a solemn looking man greeted me. He was wearing a plaid shirt, jeans, and a pair of sneakers. He appeared comfortable and sure of himself. He wasn't all dressed up, which was fine with me. The clothes people wore never impressed me. It was who the person was underneath that would do that. I introduced myself, and we went into the living room and sat down on the couch. Victor sat on my left side. I explained what Scleroderma was and showed him my hands. By observing Victor's reaction, I knew he had not realized the seriousness of my illness. He had no idea it was a deadly disease with no known cure. Victor had thought it was only a minor skin condition. Now he knew better, but his words were reassuring. He felt it would not be a problem to reverse the effects of the Scleroderma, and was confident he could restore me to complete health. I felt instant confidence in him and his belief that he would reverse my condition. I knew I should let myself have faith, and believed him.

He went on to say he would not be able to do anything for my fingers that had been fused, but could make the rest of my hand healthier, and give me more use around those fingers. He was particularly interested in my left hand, which was chronically bent. It could neither open nor completely close.

Victor liked to videotape clients when it was possible to see visual change. He was certain my healing would be obvious and make a good documentary. I had no problem with that. If he had the confidence to tape my progress, it meant he was confident that he would achieve the results he promised. He went on to say he could return my left hand to a normal state, and I would once more be able to make a fist. No one before him ever told me they could accomplish such a feat. It was hard to imagine. Now I continued the conversation, telling Victor my body was severely inflamed, and I was taking Prednisone to bring the inflammation down. He thought it a good idea to keep taking the medication, because it would make his job easier. The sooner the inflammation was under control, the quicker he could begin to heal the Scleroderma. He explained to me, when the body is more relaxed it will be easier to bring the body back to a healthier position. Healers should use any benefit that medicine can bring to their advantage. If the drug helps the inflammation, so be it. The healing process would go a lot faster and be more effective with this extra control for my pain. Victor's reasoning made sense. Other healers always wanted me off medication. I always thought if the medication were helping at all I would let it work. The sooner I saw the Scleroderma under control, the sooner I would stop taking it. Victor said he would let me know when to stop taking the Prednisone. I would be happy when that time came. In the meantime, it would help bring down the inflammation quicker than if it were just he working on me. Once again, I had no trouble believing him.

He went on to explain that his healing was accomplished through working on the bone marrow. This, he believed, was the most important part of the immune system. When the bone marrow works properly, the entire body can be healthy. He pulled his shirt- sleeve down over his right hand and covered my left hand with his own. He explained that by covering his hand this way with the proper fabric, it acts as a filter through which his healing energy could enter my body. The right fabric would make his work stronger. He reassured me he was not afraid to touch my hands even though they looked shiny and swollen. I knew instantly that Victor held more power than anyone I had met before. I felt a rush of energy run through my entire body. Although it was a more subtle sensation than I had felt with any other healer, I knew Victor was much stronger than all of them. I brimmed with confidence in the presence of his power.

*Could it be true that the Universe had finally sent me the right person, the one who could heal me, take away the pain and bring me back to health? Oh how I wished it were so, and in my heart, I believed.*

As he worked on me, I told him the many therapies I had tried, emphasizing the dental work. Before meeting me Victor was certain I would need to change my dental material, but now he praised the work, and went on to ask the name of my dentist. He wanted to go to Dr. Gershon himself, because he desired the same work for his own teeth. I was pleased with his reaction. Gary Elder had been interested in the concept, but never asked for the dentist. That was as far as it went. Martin Obel went for one visit but never followed through. Victor was the first to see how much Dr. Gershon had done for my health.

I offered to bring him a copy of the lab work the following week. By doing this, Dr. Gershon wouldn't ask if it was all right to discuss my case with him.

Victor thought my shirt and pants were fairly good, suggesting I wear the same ones the next time we met. But what really amazed him were my shoes. He looked closely at them, touching them and telling me how good they felt. "I've been looking for good shoes forever. Yours are the best I've seen. They will benefit your health."

"I discovered them in a place called Sara's Custom Shoes in Santa Fe, New Mexico." I remembered standing on a piece of paper while Sara traced my feet. I looked at the different styles, types, and colors, immediately picking the purple color in a low boot style. The boots had spoken to me, beckoning me with their soft leather and thick rubber sole. I instinctively knew I could walk in them without pain. Sara told me two months would pass before they became mine, explaining she made them by hand. I never regretted this purchase. It was well worth the wait, and the money. When they finally arrived, I put them on immediately. It was like heaven on my feet. Even with light weight socks I was able to walk for longer distances without my feet bothering me as much as they had been.

Victor's acknowledgement of my shoes was another positive sign. When we parted I was pleased with our session together, and impressed with Victor. That day there was not a miraculous change in my body, although I could tell things were beginning to move around. I felt totally confident that I had indeed found the person who would heal me. I truly believed he would do as he said; restore me once again to perfect health. We made an appointment for the following week.

Deborah and Heidi were amazed at my strong, positive feelings. Instead of laughter, they found me serious in my trust. Michael was not surprised. He was glad he had brought us together, believing Victor was a true healer. But he was interested in my opinion concerning Victor's self image. I told Michael I had no problem that he believed in himself. To me it was a display of his power, he was being aware of the truth. I respected people who had a definite opinion. Victor certainly did. I was glad it was similar to my own outlook. I respected the fact that Victor knew he had real healing powers and let everyone know it. I felt he was the real thing. Compared to him, the other healers had insignificant abilities. Michael believed both Victor and myself had much in common. He was right.

My body felt better the day after my first treatment. Emotionally I was stronger because I had found someone to believe in. That night I slept sounder than I had in months. I had hardly any joint pain. When moving around in my sleep, I didn't wake up as in the past. It was such a relief to finally find the person who could really heal me. It became a joy just to get a good night's rest. When I awoke the next morning I wasn't my usual stiff self, and could get out of bed and walk with more ease. I noticed a big difference in my physical improvement. Previously, one of my fused fingers began to get a red line over the knuckle area. This indicated the beginning of an infection. The morning after my treatment the redness almost disappeared and my left hand was able to close more than it had in a while.

The next day I went out and bought the quilts Victor had suggested. I bought one to cover the mattress, one for on top of the bed and one to make into a pillow. I also bought three quilts to use on my son's bed plus a few pillow shams. I even bought a quilt to place over my couch in the living room. Since I spent so much time sitting there it should be healthy too. Of course it didn't match with the rest of the décor. My couch was of leopard print velvet, which now was draped with a blue, white and yellow striped quilt. A new fashion statement, maybe? It didn't matter what it looked like. Being healthy was my main concern. If I were going to do something I would do it right. If Victor believed that sleeping on a particular quilt helped the healing process, I would buy the quilt. None of this was difficult. He had explained the importance of the right fabric regarding the immune system, and said it would support an anti-inflammatory reaction, especially for my disease. These were the best quilts he could find, and he wanted to be certain I bought them while they were currently in the stores. Michael had told Victor I would do whatever was asked of me in the healing process. Of course I would. I went to him to be healed, so why should I do anything else, particularly after all this time. I didn't want to compromise his work. He wasn't trying invasive procedures. He wasn't telling me to stop my medication. He said nothing about vitamins or diet. If sleeping on a certain quilt and wearing special clothes made a difference, it was easy enough to try it. Willingly, I would do whatever it took to reverse the Scleroderma. I was sure Victor would be able to do this for me, and was going to do whatever he asked. Victor explained if everyone around me were healthy, it would make a good impact on my health and would help his work on me. To help with my healing process the entire family was going to sleep on healthy bedding and wear healthy t-shirts. If I was to be healthy, everyone around me had to be healthy too. I even bought quilts for my parents.

At the end of my first appointment Victor said he would bring me a sweatshirt made from the best material. He wanted me to wear it to give a positive influence to my body. His instruction was to wash it at night and wear it every day. I went through my closet and filled a bag with t-shirts, wanting Victor to look at them for approval. Anything that might adversely affect my health would go out with the trash.

By my next appointment I once again felt pain in my body,

but not nearly as strong as before. I couldn't wait for another treatment.

**Victor:** When Michael told me about his friend, Jane, he didn't explain to me how sick she was. He just told me she had some sickness with the skin. I was not interested in taking on any new clients unless I would get some new information for my research. I thought any skin cream or medical doctor could take care of the problem. Even though Michael knew I wasn't really interested, he kept pushing me to see her. He continued calling and asking me for over two months. I thought if I would say, "wear certain clothes" or "repair your teeth" she would never come to see me. But Michael kept calling back and telling me she was willing to wear any clothes I said. She had her teeth repaired years ago. I told him nobody knows how to repair teeth correctly. If she really wants to work with me she will repair them again. He came back again and said if she needed to she would even do the dental work over. I had never seen such an agreeable person. She just had a little skin problem and she said she would do anything I asked her to. Finally, I gave in and decided to meet her. I told Michael she could call and arrange an appointment. She called me and we set up a time to meet at Michael's apartment.

When I first saw Jane I understood the extensive damage of this disease. It was not at all what I expected, not even close. And when she showed me her hands, I knew this was a disease useful for both research and documentation. The hand damage was very severe, the right hand was fused in all the middle knuckle joints, the left hand was totally bent. Both her hands looked like rakes. It was a visual sickness that resembled arthritis, but much more inflamed. I knew exactly how to work on arthritis, and didn't believe this would be very difficult. If one could be reversed, why not the other.

Jane explained how devastating this disease was. There

were no treatments to cure Scleroderma, and was told by the doctors it was hopeless to reverse the damage already done to the bones and muscles. There was no long term hope for anyone who had Systemic Scleroderma. People who are diagnosed with Scleroderma usually don't live too long. This information excited me. It gave me a chance to prove my method of regeneration of a deadly disease by working on the bone marrow. I could also use my research and theories concerning the importance of the right materials and dental work. I was very confident about my knowledge. Jane was the perfect person to work with because she had promised to cooperate and do whatever I asked to make her well.

I began my work, beginning by placing my hand over the inflamed area. This brings the inflammation down by sending anti-inflammatory frequency from my healthy hands into her skin and bones. I felt a huge amount of pain, intoxication and inflammation moving throughout her body. But what impressed me the most was that Jane's teeth caused neither pain nor blockage. It was the first time I had seen teeth in good condition after having a large amount of dental repairs. The high quality of her dental work surprised me, revising my opinion that her teeth would be the biggest problem. I always had trouble with my own teeth, but now believed Dr. Gershon might be the one to fix them. I had to work on my mouth daily to make sure nothing bothered me while helping a client.

Before meeting Jane, I didn't know what her attitude might be concerning clothes. In the past I worked with people who didn't understand the importance of wearing clothing with the proper frequency. It was difficult to heal someone if the materials they wore stood in the way. I never want to just help a condition. I always want to completely fix the health problem or immune system condition and send people on their healthy way. People should not have to keep coming back to me for treatments. It's better to be healthy and just call me to say hello then to continue coming to see me because you are sick. I explained to Jane how dependent health and bone marrow could be on the proper clothing. Most clients wore the recommended clothes only for the time of the treatments. It made my work easier when I saw them, but as soon as they went home, they would change. This interrupted all the work I had just completed. Women complained, "Victor, you need to find clothes that look more feminine and have some style." At the time only a few men's t-shirts and sweatshirts felt good. Most people spend their lives wearing clothes that have a negative effect on their body and never even realize it. I always tell anyone that will listen, it is cheaper to buy the right clothes along with the right bedding than to spend money on healers and doctors.

Back to Jane... I bought extra shirts and sweaters for someone like Jane. The sweatshirt for her was made from the best material I could find. Jane said she would wear only what I told her. I was so happy I didn't need to fight and convince her about that. For the first time my job could begin in the right way from the start. Even after giving her the sweatshirt I wasn't sure if she would actually wear it all the time. People always thought they could wear different clothing behind my back and I wouldn't know about it. They couldn't believe that I actually felt the difference. It was always apparent to me that they had been wearing the wrong clothes when they were not with me. No one else had worn only the clothes I had suggested. They always blamed me for not finding enough clothes that they thought were stylish and would wear all the time. To me this was a foolish attitude. Wasn't your health more important to you than the way you looked? Hoping Jane would wear only what I told her, I thought, "We will see." With all the time I had spent explaining to people about clothes, not many had listened or really understood the importance.

The following week I gave Jane the sweatshirt and she immediately put it on. When I saw her a week later she was in the same sweatshirt and brought a bag of clothes from her closet for me to test. Finally someone was co-operative which could only make my work easier. Jane also told me she was using an anti-inflammatory medication. I felt very confident that this medication would not interrupt her immune system. Jane asked me if she should continue the medication or stop it right away. She told me she had worked with other healers before. They had always wanted her to stop any medication she was taking. I told her this medication was very good. It could only help my work. This anti- inflammatory medicine together with my anti-inflammatory knowledge could bring about much faster results. When her body felt strong enough, I would be the first to have her speak to her doctor about stopping it. She agreed, and we continued to work.

I didn't want to scare Jane about her condition. Being on medication, she wasn't fully aware concerning the danger facing her body. Her system was close to collapsing, but I knew after working together she would improve. After that I could tell her how serious the condition had been. Jane always believed she could beat this disease, but in the past no one ever had. She said she would not only survive it, she would be back to the health she had before she got this disease. I wondered about her, and thought she must be blind. Didn't she see her hands? Her inflammation? She had a strange attitude. One I had never seen before, but it got to me. In truth she really didn't know if I could reverse this disease, but believed my promise to do just that. After the first treatment, I believed the Scleroderma was reversible, but Jane's time and full co-operation was needed.

While I worked on her, Jane asked me why I pulled the sleeve of my shirt over my own hand before touching her hand. Maybe she thought I was afraid to touch her. I explained that healing bone marrow works like an exchange of energy information. The material between our hands becomes a filter in both directions. A fabric that has health frequency information helps to direct my work positively. It would clear the inflammatory influence that was coming from her hand into my hand while I worked and make my work more efficient. A lot of the inflammatory frequency coming out of her hands and body would not be picked up into mine. If I worked without the fabric her inflammatory influence would have a much stronger effect on the job I was doing. Her pain symptoms would strongly affect my hands and body and I could lose the path of clear health frequency. The fabric that is covering my hand gives me a better sense of this direction. The amount of time necessary for treatment to make a real change in a serious disease can take several hours. During the first hour I usually just clear a small area from the disease information that is all over the body. Only after making a small area a lot healthier can the rest of the body respond. The brain immediately receives this new information. All of our immune systems have an original blueprint of health. The body wants to return to this condition and start producing the right signals and the right chemistry that will spread all over from this healthy area. After almost two hours of working through Jane's hand, I could start sending information further than just this small area I had cleaned out. Through experience, my hands have developed the ability to immediately give me information as to which area I should start working. Sometimes I start on the hands, sometimes the feet, sometimes around the neck or head area. With Jane, after working on her hand I went to the back of her neck. This area is most important to the information going into and out of the brain. When I clear this area, the healthy information can flow in both directions.

I had touched her hands when we first met, wanting her

to know I was not afraid to catch her disease. It's important to be gentle at first meeting. People with a skin disease or other visible impairments can be sensitive about scaring people with their appearance.

While working on Jane I recalled an experience with a man who had gangrene in his leg. I had never seen anything like it. His skin was broken making it possible to see his muscles with liquid protruding from the opening. He had black toes and muscles that were completely dead. Much to his doctor's amazement, I reversed the gangrene. This removed any fears I may have harbored concerning the appearance of a sick person. Nothing had made a stronger impression on me. Now the one thing that impresses me more is that people are ignorant of the fact that almost all diseases are reversible.

**Jane:** When I saw Victor the next week, I told him about all the improvements I had felt right away. He was happy that I had felt results after one time. He told me that with a lot of time and effort, this disease would be easy for him to change. I had faith in his abilities that he would be able to change my health back to normal. He wasn't aware of the fact that no one had previously had any real cure for Scleroderma. This didn't matter to him, or change the fact that I thought he would cure me. He was happy that I brought him the information about Dr. Gershon and the shoes. Victor said that even without wearing the right clothes, the dental work and the shoes I had been wearing had helped me tremendously. These had helped the condition move more quickly towards healing. I was alive because I had done the right things before meeting him. Even though my body was very inflamed by the time we met, I would have been in much worse shape without all the work done before. Victor told me the dental work had saved my life, and gave me the time needed to find him. He gave me a sweatshirt in very good fabric. It didn't look that much different than a lot of other sweatshirts. I went in the other room and took off the shirt I was wearing and put on the good one. It felt really nice and comfortable. If he thought it would help heal my disease I would wear it. It didn't bother my skin, it was a nice color blue, and I was happy wearing sweatshirts anyway. It was cold outside and the cold and damp always bothered me. If it would keep me warm while it was helping me get healthy, that was fine with me. I thought it was really generous of Victor to give his clients clothes without asking for repayment. He felt that in the long run it made his job easier. It would save him time and energy he would otherwise use in fighting the bad materials the client was wearing. I showed Victor the shirts from home. He dismissed a few, but was surprised that most of them were quite good. Placing the bad ones in a separate pile to throw out, I made a mental note to bring a bag of clothes to each appointment so that Victor could check my entire wardrobe. I wanted to follow his routine, do it right, and not do anything that would adversely effect his curing me of Scleroderma. My plan was to wear the sweatshirt every day until my next appointment. I would wash it at night so it would be clean the next day. I didn't care about wearing the same thing everyday. I wanted to be healthy.

In the week following our first meeting, I felt much better. My left hand had started becoming more flexible and bending more. My shoulders were working more and with less pain. The inflammation had gone down right after Victor first worked on me. After a few days, the pain gradually returned but not as bad as before the treatment. The redness in my fused finger was almost all gone. It was getting infected before I saw Victor, but now there was no indication of any problem. The results after only one session thrilled me. Unfortunately, I only had the financial means to see him once a week. Though he charged less than some other healers and was much more powerful, there was only so much we could afford. I knew my progress could move a lot faster if we had more time together, but Victor assured me he would make me well despite this limitation.

Victor continued working the same way, seated on my left, always beginning with my left hand. This was his main focal point, wanting my bone marrow to work normally, as soon as possible. He would work that way for a while, then move his hand to different areas as he felt a change in where he was working. Most of the time he held his hand over mine, but he would also place his hand on the back of my neck or shoulder area, and sometimes my knee. There was a feeling of energy flowing into my body from his hand, although it was difficult to actually describe the sensation. It started out subtly, but then intensified as the time went by. By the end of our session, I felt as if I was walking up in the clouds.

After a few appointments, the color and texture of my hands improved. The flexibility in my body was better than it had been for a long time. The fingers on my left hand were beginning to curl closer to my palm, but I was still inflamed. Victor told me to continue taking the Prednisone. He would let me know when I should stop. In the meantime, it would make his job quicker to have the help of the anti-inflammatory. After five years of being in pain and discomfort, I was finally feeling much better. Not only was the physical pain better, I was optimistic about finding the one person who I knew would really heal me totally. No one before him had given me any kind of reason for my condition. He had explanations about everything that had affected my health up until meeting him. He had a plan on how to change all of the influence the Scleroderma had caused to my body. By the way I felt inside and the observable changes in my skin color and hands, I was sure Victor was the real thing. I had been going in the right direction in my search for complete health, and hadn't stopped looking until I found an answer. Victor was the first true healer I had ever met. I was seeing real results right from the start. There was no doubt in my mind when he said he would return me to complete health.

**VICTOR:** After seeing Jane during the day, I lay on my bed remembering other days, other people, and other places.

Very often the people who came to me for treatment would tell me about their disease. I could feel the disease as it was described to me. Diseases differ from one another, but my mind could memorize the feelings of each illness, and started to recognize the differences. When I worked I detected different feelings through my hands. Some sensations even entered my body, sometimes my organs. In the beginning these sensations were strange. Later I understood, realizing it was like mixing two cups of water together. One cup filled with dirty water, the other cup has clear, clean water. The cup with the clear water is continually filled from a clean source. After a time of mixing these two waters, all the water will be clear. Sometimes it takes a long time to wash away all the dirt, but eventually it will happen. Inflammatory processes in the body also have their own feelings. They differ from one condition to another. One condition may have more lymph fat surrounding the inflamed places. Others have no fat. Sometimes the areas are too hot and don't want to accept any correction in the frequency. These areas are like black holes.

My thoughts returned to Jane and the dedication she showed in her desire to heal and be well. In thinking about it, if her willingness to adhere to all that I asked of her were true, she would be the first to do so.

I remembered a trip to Philadelphia to visit a friend. We were driving back to his house when he stopped to drop something off with an acquaintance. When he returned to the car he was very upset. He told me his friend was paralyzed from the neck down, and it pained him to see someone he cared for in such condition. He thought it would be a miracle if anyone could help this man. I said, "Let's go back. Paralysis is one of the easiest conditions to change." In Russia, I worked on a few people who were partially paralyzed. I knew the mechanics involved, and didn't think it would be a bigger problem to alter someone who was fully paralyzed. It would just take more time. My friend was skeptical, "Victor, nobody can repair spinal cord injuries." I knew I could. We returned to the house of the paralyzed man. He was American, but spoke fairly good Russian, making it easier for me. He had been injured in an automobile accident fourteen years before, and been paralyzed from the neck down. The doctors had put a metal rod in his neck. I told him I could help, but it might take a year.

"Okay, let's start working."

My friend brought his video camera so we could tape the injured man right from the beginning. I decided to put all my time and effort into this healing. He promised me a large sum of money after I returned movement to his arms and hands. For me, it was important for the world to see that paralysis could be cured. This required many hours of work each day. His progress moved quickly. Once again the importance of wearing the right materials became apparent to me. There was a noticeable difference in my work depending on the clothing he wore, but at this time I still didn't fully realize the importance of the mattress. When he lay on his water mattress my work was all right, but definitely more effective when he sat in a chair.

After a time some feeling returned, and he felt pressure below his chest and in his arms. He was making rapid progress. By a month and a half he could control movement in his torso. It was now possible to watch him move forward and back, along with a moving motion that went from side to side at his waist. He was impressed. The shoulder area also progressed. He could move his shoulders back and forth. When I lifted his arm in an upward position and held his hand, he was able to pull down with great strength while I held on to him. In this posture, he could slightly lift his body. The back and biceps started working. His breathing was one of the first areas to improve. Within two months his muscle tone as well as his skin color changed for the better.

I returned to New York to earn enough money to pay my living expenses. In my absence no treatment was administered to the paralyzed patient. I was gone for two weeks. Upon returning to Philadelphia I worked on him for four and a half hours. He now had more control over movement in his arms. Everything was videotaped. Once again I returned to New York. Two days went by when I received a call from my patient's friend. What he told me came as a shock. "My friend does not want to work with you anymore." He did not want to progress any further or put so much time into his rehabilitation. Why was this happening? Why wouldn't the paralyzed man speak directly to me? I had been so excited, so filled with hope. In just two months time I changed most of his difficulty. His condition was clear to me. It would not take a great deal of effort to make him well. Now his friend was saying in no uncertain terms that the man would not even speak to me. All of my joy and expectations were broken. I couldn't understand it. I showed the videotapes to a doctor, explaining the work already done. The doctor was impressed with the results he saw on the tape and called the man on the telephone, wanting to know why he stopped working with me. The man refused to talk about it. Four or five months went by. Then one day my phone rang. Once again the paralyzed man wanted help. He said he was having stomach problems, and also asked for a copy of the videotape. I refused both his requests, no longer trusting him to finish the work we had started. He was not only damaging himself, but he prevented knowledge that others would be happy to receive. He once told me that his dream was to have his hands become strong enough to be able to squeeze a woman. If he had only given me another few months he could have squeezed all the girls he liked. Now his offer came too late. I knew he would never let me finish the job, and could not prove my knowledge to the medical community.

I sighed. It was a painful memory, and realized I was making comparisons between then and now. Everything had started so well with Jane. My one wish was that it would end as well. But I was getting ahead of myself. I only wanted Jane to heal, and I would try to make it so.

Jane: I told Dr. Horowitz when I began my sessions with Victor. He had seen no improvement with either one of my previous healers, but after working for a few weeks with Victor, Dr. Horowitz believed I was in remission. He wasn't sure there could be much more improvement, and felt satisfied if there was no more deterioration. He didn't really think I would be completely healed. No one had successfully reversed the damages Scleroderma could cause. I wanted him to know about the work I was doing with Victor. In that way he could see that real changes were taking place. I was determined to return to complete health from the first diagnosis of Scleroderma. The doctor had followed my trials of alternative therapies right from the start. I wasn't going to stop showing him I could return to health, especially now that Victor was in my life. If I found the right things to do, Dr. Horowitz might use them to help other patients in a similar condition. There was no reason to hide any cure I could find. If other people could avoid the pain I went through, why shouldn't my knowledge be shared.

During our early sessions together, Victor could see the minimal range of motion in my arms and shoulders. There was no twisting movement in either my arms or wrists. My elbows could not straighten, and when I awoke each morning, my body still ached. After every treatment, there were small improvements. I lived in constant pain, but less than before. Once again Victor said he would tell me when to stop the Prednisone. Though listening to him, I was still anxious to go off the medication. When I was finally down to taking just 2.5 mg. a day, he suggested discussing the situation with Dr. Horowitz. After checking my blood work, the doctor agreed that the inflammation seemed to be gone and the medication could stop. It was now the beginning of March, and the first time in over six years I was taking nothing. No medication. No vitamins. I hadn't taken any vitamins since I had stopped by myself over a year ago. I discussed with Victor if there were any vitamins or supplements that would help his work along. I wasn't sure what he thought about vitamins.

Victor told me there was one supplement I needed to take regularly. It is a combination of calcium, magnesium and a little vitamin C. He thought everyone should be taking this supplement. He felt it was especially important for me at this stage of my illness and for my age. Calcium can keep your bones and your general health in good shape. Almost a year before I met Victor, Dr. Horowitz had recommended that I take a calcium supplement. He suggested an over-the-counter brand. I didn't feel right going into a drug store and just buying a brand name, and looked into the vitamin companies whose products I had used in the past. I tried a few different brands and ingredient combinations. None of them felt right to my body and I stopped taking them all very quickly. Victor had tested many different calcium supplements and found one that worked well, with no negative side effects. I had faith in his research and knowledge and was willing to give it a try. I ordered it immediately and started taking it. The experts recommended calcium and magnesium to help you sleep, so I worked it into my evening routine. I'm still taking it at night, and feel it is still helping my body.

**Victor:** Jane told me her entire story about all the vitamins that she had been taking. She had gone to a very good nutritionist at the start of her illness. When she started taking all the supplements her body and her immune system reacted positively. Her body was not in a healthy condition. She was not in a stage where her body wouldn't be able to digest anything that wasn't totally right. For a while the supplements that had been recommended seemed to help. The nutritionist switched her to different brands of vitamins. These supplements must have been more appropriate for her body. The dosage she suggested worked well. It is important to know that it is not just the brand that you take. How much you are taking is equally important. Even the good positive effects of vitamins can become damaging if you take too much. Some people think if they take a lot more than the recommended dosage, it will help you more. This can damage you as easily as many toxins. If you are taking the wrong vitamins, even the recommended dosage can damage you. At times even the wrong combination of vitamins can cause a negative reaction. If your body is lacking in a certain vitamin, your immune system can handle just a small amount and in a short period of time. This information will give direction and support to the immune system. The body and the immune system will very quickly store the right vitamins, the right direction and the right information. If you start overloading this, the body develops an allergic reaction to the vitamin you are taking in excess of what you need. This might show up first in the stomach, causing a nauseated feeling that many people have and don't relate to the vitamins they are taking. It can also affect the intestines, and spread to other conditions you might not associate with taking vitamins.

**JANE:** My hands were more flexible and my skin quality was much better. In the past few years my skin had turned a strange yellow color, only now did it start returning to a normal skin tone. There was also a noticeable difference in the quality of my skin. It no longer had a shiny textured look. My fingers were not only bending more, they were also becoming straighter. I felt better than I had in years.

I acquired more healthy clothing. Some were given to me from Victor, and when he told me about anything good he found, I made sure to buy it myself. Feeling better and wanting to keep my healing going in the right direction, kept me as obsessed as Victor about wearing only the right materials. Everything he had suggested so far was working. I wanted to keep it that way. There was no reason to doubt what he was telling me. Dr. Horowitz thought I was doing great, definitely in remission. He could see the difference in my skin within two weeks of my starting to work with Victor.

In the middle of March, my husband and I were invited to a formal wedding. Since working with Victor, I only wore my healthy clothes. Wearing a sweatshirt, jeans and purple boots to a formal affair was out of the question. When I told Victor about attending this party, he was not happy because he knew that my clothes would be less than perfect. I had no choice. After searching the Mall, a beaded top along with a pair of satin pants became my outfit for the evening. Nothing seemed particularly healthy, but I needed something dressy. I owned a pair of high heel shoes that were fairly comfortable, and decided to wear them. Knowing I wasn't doing the right thing for my body did not deter me, believing one evening in the wrong clothes would not make much difference. How wrong I was. My feet bothered me before we even reached the hotel where the wedding was held. I constantly removed my shoes due to great discomfort. A necklace of my own design, consisting of large tourmaline beads decorated my neck. It never bothered me before, but now my neck began to hurt, and the necklace had to be removed and placed carefully in my bag. Two hours into the evening, my back left tooth began hurting me. I couldn't believe it, having never experienced a toothache before. It became unbearably painful. So much so, by the end of the evening I was in agony and couldn't wait to get home and out of my clothes. I hoped the pain would disappear after getting undressed, never believing it could continue through the night and into the following day. The next morning, my toothache still had not gone away. I wanted to wait before calling the dentist, but the pain was too great. Dr. Gershon told me to come in the following morning. I had just seen him two weeks earlier for a check up. At that time there were no problems in my mouth. He now looked at the painful tooth and took an X-ray. He found a large pocket of infection under the left wisdom tooth. Dr. Gershon could not understand where it came from, believing by the size of the infection it certainly would have been noticed from our last appointment. When I told him it was from wearing the wrong clothes, he laughed. But when he looked at me, it was obvious I was serious. (I had told him about Victor, my new healer, when I first started working with him. At the time Dr. Gershon looked at me skeptically, and I think he might have been a little worried after his experience with Martin, the last healer. I had assured Dr. Gershon that Victor was the real thing, and would not give him any of the craziness that Martin had. After meeting Victor, he realized I was right in my assessment, and agreed to help Victor with his research.) My body had been cleansed by wearing healthy clothes, and when I dressed in clothing made from bad fabrics, even for only one night, there was an instant reaction. My tooth became infected, and it needed to be pulled. I had never lost a tooth before, never even needed my wisdom teeth removed. I wore bad clothes for one evening and needed a tooth pulled a few days later. That was a pretty strong sign that I had better wear only healthy clothes from then on. Many people heard my story of wearing the wrong clothing and losing a tooth. A few friends looked at me as if I was crazy, but those who knew me well, understood my belief as to the real cause of what happened. I learn my lessons quickly, and this was a major experience that did not need repeating.

Victor liked the story, appreciating the fact that I knew the incident occurred because of the clothing, and especially the wrong shoes. He believed that shoes were often the key to dental problems. I think for the first time he recognized my agreement with conclusions he had come to believe through his many years of research. I meant what I said about doing whatever it took to heal me, and now he saw that my intentions were completely serious.

I continued to work with Victor once a week in person. He usually called me two or three other times during the week in order to work on me via the telephone. I found it interesting that the healing process could possibly work this way. He always asked me in which hand I held the receiver. We worked that way for a while, even though my arm and hand holding the receiver would start to get numb. He wouldn't let me switch hands until he felt he was ready to work on the other side. Only then would he tell me to switch hands. Sometimes we talked, but usually there was silence between us as he did what he was doing. Often his television was playing in the background. On one occasion I heard a lot of shouting, and asked Victor what he was watching. You can imagine my surprise when he said it was The Jerry Springer show. That type of program never struck me as being particularly healing. Victor said it was good. He worked better because he found it funny. I thought he had a strange sense of humor, but if it made him laugh it must have served some purpose, one I did not understand.

When we worked by telephone, I felt my body breathing in the same sensations I experienced while seated next to him.

**Victor:** People ask how I can work by telephone. Can changes really occur in the body across telephone lines? I discovered that many inflammatory processes were easier to change in this manner, just as bringing down a temperature also became simpler. But the best results occurred with people who had pneumonia or gangrene. It also was apparent to me if the client wore the right clothing, whether he or she was lying down or comfortably seated, and even the type of bedding they used. The condition of the person's teeth also became apparent. Teeth problems can bother me a great deal when working by phone. I lost a few of my own teeth before discovering the source of such discomfort. After that, I knew I had to be careful while working over the telephone.

The inflammatory process is easier to change through the phone because you are far away from the aura (energy field) of the sick person. The greater the distance between the person and myself, the better the results. From my home in Russia I worked on a few people living in America. One woman had bad circulation in one arm due to an injury. Her arm and hand were always freezing. I worked on her by telephone. She was shocked when her circulation returned warming the area that was once so very cold.

I always ask the client in which hand they are holding the telephone, needing to know if it is their right or left hand. I begin by working from the person's healthier side, wanting to make this side even stronger. This strategy makes my work much more effective. Once it has reached maximum strength, it can help push the inflammation away and give the body direction. It also signals the immune system to be healthy. When the immune system is directed from the outside it responds more easily through the healthier space.

My method is based on this theory. I begin the work on the one space that I feel is healthiest and gives the best response. From this space I organize the entire body and force it to work against the problem. When the body is healthy in one place it wants to share this information with the entire body, and push away everything that doesn't feel right. The telephone work is important because I am giving healthy information from my body. The person holding the telephone on the other end of the line is responding to this information.

It is common for most people to pick up the telephone receiver with their left hand. This can cause problems. You don't know the condition of the person who is calling, and when you use your left hand, information is coming to you not only by sound but also through the frequency field of the other person. When you hold the receiver the frequency goes through the left arm, through the left shoulder and to the heart, which is located on the left side. If you hold the receiver in your right hand, the blood stream and body mass have enough space to filter this information before it gets to the heart. There is less chance that you will pick up a condition from the other person. Without even realizing it you can feel the condition of the person on the other end of the line. No matter how healthy you are, if the person on the other side has a heart condition you can receive these signaling feelings in your own heart. Your body is not prepared, and it is possible to have a heart attack right away. This is because the difference between the person's heart that is calling and your heart is so tremendous it can work as a severe shock to a healthy heart.

While working on Jane through the telephone I told her a brief story from my practice. Nadia was a healthy person, and always followed my suggestions. One day while sitting in her living room, the telephone rang and she ran to get it. She picked up the receiver in her left hand and began speaking. Within five or ten seconds she cried out, "Victor, I feel a pain in my heart. It's hurting so much." I told her to switch hands instantly, saying the person on the other end may have a heart problem. Nadia threw the phone down, exclaiming the person calling had just returned from the hospital after having repairs done to her heart. Nadia learned her lesson and from that time on used only her right hand to pick up the phone. I hoped Jane would do the same.

**Jane:** By the middle of April I felt a big difference in my body. At the beginning of all my strange symptoms, I developed a new ability. For the past six years I was able to tell if it was going to rain. A day or two before the snow or rain arrived my joints ached in a way that felt different from the usual aches and pains. It had been difficult for me to understand how people with arthritis could feel the rain coming. It made no sense to me. I found out the hard way just how easy it is to predict the oncoming storms. Now my body felt good when the weather was nice, but still developed minor aches the day before it rained. They were not nearly as bad as before. Sometimes there were days upon opening my eyes when I was surprised to see the rain, having had no indication it was coming. That truly amazed me.

I felt stronger than ever. The muscles in my arms were filling out, becoming strengthened, more solid. Both wrists, once thin and weak during my years of deteriorating health, were gradually returning to their previous appearance. Victor encouraged me to take walks. At first I couldn't go very far or for any length of time, but slowly it became easier. In a week or two, my walks were faster and for longer distances. My joints did not hurt as they once did, but there were times my muscles ached. I did not mind this new aching, knowing it was only because my body was not used to all the walking.

My hands were getting better, becoming stronger. Even my fingers were bending more, opening and closing without enormous effort. The color of my skin gradually improved. The texture looked smoother, less scaly. I didn't realize that my face had also undergone a change for the better. My looks had altered glaringly from the start of the disease, so much so that my face became almost unrecognizable to me. Because of this I had stayed away from mirrors. It was depressing to look too closely at the face that looked back at me. Now that I felt better, it was easier to examine myself. It amazed me to see my lips regaining their shape. At the beginning of my illness, my top lip became only a line on my face. I showed Victor a picture of myself before the Scleroderma invaded me. He said I would one day look that way again. I was almost afraid to believe him, because counting on it, might bring me disappointment. But now my mouth was beginning to fill out, and look like my lips once again. This made a great impression on me. The tightness of my skin in every part of my body was disappearing. My entire body was finally relaxing into a healthier state.

It was now May. Dr. Horowitz believed the Scleroderma was definitely in remission.

*I wanted to ask the doctor if he thought my body could return to what it had once been. I had worked so hard, waited so long, gone through so much. How his words would sting me if he uttered what I could not bear to hear. But I had to ask, had to know.*

"Do you think I will return to my original state? I know my body is feeling good." Dr. Horowitz had never discouraged me in my search for answers, but he knew the disease had never before been reversed. He looked at me skeptically and offered only silence. He knew me well enough not to tell me I couldn't accomplish this return to health.

**Victor:** When I told Jane about the healthy quilts she quickly went to buy a few, discovering stores in Westchester that carried them. I wanted to buy all the quilts that were in the stores. They were closer to a health frequency than any I had seen on the market.

**Jane:** Victor and I drove around, stopping at innumerable stores looking for a particular quilt made uniquely for one department store. The store had been taken over, and the new owners were selling all the old merchandise. We wanted to buy all the quilts that were available before we were no longer able to find them. I bought eight quilts and a few pillow shams. Even though Victor had bought over a hundred of them already, he also bought more on our travels. Buying so many might have appeared strange to friends and family, but I wanted to make certain there were enough for the people I loved.

While driving in the car together, Victor related stories to me from the past. One of these tales concerned Chernobyl.

After the tragedy at Chernobyl, a friend of Victor's took three turns in helping to cleanse that poisonous place. The government was paying good money to entice workers for clean up duty. The pay was much higher than anyone received from a regular job, so Victor's friend illegally managed to get himself hired three times instead of the one time permitted by the government. These workers received no protective clothing except for an old pair of gloves. The friend didn't care about the dangerous conditions, he only knew he was making more money then he ever believed possible. When Victor saw his friend four years later, he discovered he was sick. Neither his bone marrow nor his blood worked properly. The doctors told him he was in the early stages of Leukemia, and his thyroid was not good. Victor worked on his friend wanting to improve his health. When the time came for his next blood test, he immediately showed signs of improvement. But the most pronounced changes took place when Victor worked with his friend by telephone. He was able to clean out much of the radiation effect that inhabited his friend's body. Victor believed that in this case working through the phone was more effective then being physically close to him. His friend related stories about the people living in Chernobyl. He explained that during the winter, families all used fire wood to warm their homes. Most of the wood came from the area filled with radiation. After the wood had fully burned, the ashes were cleaned from the fireplace, and thrown into the back yard where the vegetable gardens were planted. The people then ate the food, making each backyard and every fireplace a miniature Chernobyl.

At the time of Chernobyl Victor was working in Siberia. They never had good chocolate candy there. Now, out of the blue, chocolates began arriving and were sold in the company store. These chocolates didn't feel right to Victor. He looked to see where they came from; imported from BelaRussia, an area near Chernobyl. Victor did not eat them.

People left Chernobyl along with their furniture, so all the radiation moved with them. Some families, wanting to get out quickly, left their cars behind. But thieves entered the town, stripped the cars, and sold the parts. This sent radiation throughout Russia.

Others remained, and still live and work in Chernobyl. They do not want to leave. It is their home, the place where they grew up, and where they will probably die.

I liked hearing Victor's stories about Russia. It was such a different reality. It intrigued me. Until now, Chernobyl was just a place struck by disaster. Now it was real, held new meaning to me, because Victor's story had brought it to life.

Everyone could see that my condition was in fact reversing. My progress was undeniable. My arms were now much more flexible, I could raise them higher and higher without all the aches and pains. They easily moved above shoulder level. This was an enormous improvement from hardly any movement at all. By June, my legs were stronger. It was easier to straighten them, and climbing the stairs was no longer a major ordeal. At the beginning of my work with Victor, this was a problem. I had to get both feet on one step before gingerly going on to the next, stopping between each step, whether going up or down. This was no longer the case. Now I could walk the steps without resting in between. My other new accomplishment was standing up after being seated for a long period of time. Before, my body always remained stiff, and after standing, had to pause a minute or two before moving. Now I could stand up and walk right away. The flexibility and range of motion in my arms was continuing to improve. My hands were getting fuller from the developing muscles. My fingers, once thin and weak, made the knuckles look more swollen. Now my hands were becoming natural looking. The right hand that had twice gone through surgery was now more flexible at the wrist. The muscles around the wrists and arms were filling out. One of the things that made me happiest was having less pain in my legs while I slept. During the past few years I was never comfortable while sleeping. I was always awakened by pain while changing positions. Only now was my sleep restful. Upon opening my eyes I stretched my legs without the former pain, though still haunted by minimal discomfort. The first time I woke up and stretched out my body without any pain, I was in heaven. It was a long forgotten pleasure to wake up and stretch. The most insignificant things were now the most appreciated. Being able to wake up and stretch out without pain was the greatest feeling in the world to me.

Within another week or two I could finally raise my arms over my head, allowing me to undress as I had in the past. This required crossing my arms and lifting the shirt over my head. It was another major accomplishment of a seemingly ordinary task. I had an entirely different outlook on what was important in life. Good health was certainly at the top of my list. I was very happy about all the differences that were happening and felt I was definitely going in the direction of complete reversal of this disease.

*It was finally happening. After years of doctors, medication and pain, I knew my body was healing. Was Victor the last piece of the puzzle? Was this the last part of my journey? I hoped so…*

**Victor:** When people are together and share everything they can often become the same. If there is a big difference in health, it is possible to make each other sick. Continued negative influence over a long period of time makes it impossible for the immune system to defend itself. It is constantly receiving the wrong direction. When one person in a relationship is healthy and the other one isn't, eventually they will both become unhealthy. The sick person has to desire becoming well, otherwise everyone around them will be negatively affected.

There are times when emotional contact can relate to the disease process. I had a client with a sister who had breast cancer. She worried the same might happen to her. After working on her, I suggested she see Dr. Gershon for dental repairs. Changing the dental condition is always the first step. At our next appointment, she spoke of her relationship to her sister. They constantly argued. She said it was impossible for the two of them to get along because her sister was nasty, and their time together always resulted in a fight. A whole year could pass without a word spoken between them. Whenever they communicated by telephone, the conversation ended in anger and frustration. Once she had told me about this relationship and her fear of contracting breast cancer, I realized her problem. Whenever she spoke to her sister, she picked up a cancer frequency. The conversation always upset her because she was connecting with her sister only through negativity. My client was healthy and strong. She was sending both healthy information and power to her sister. She was sending frequency to her sister even just thinking about her. The sister was sick and responding with nastiness. She was sending cancer frequency information back through the power she received from conversing with the healthy sister. This became a closed cycle. They had no way to break this negative information being transferred back and forth between them. I asked her, "Do you want to be healthier? Do you want your sister to be healthier and happier?" My suggestion; "Don't speak to each other for awhile." I went on to say she should try not to think about her sister. Because of their connection, even thinking about her is the same as using a telephone. Thoughts themselves can become a conscious frequency connection. I spoke to her, emphasizing the need to disconnect the sister's body from her own power. "Her body will find a way to work on itself. Both you and your sister will be healthier because the cycle will be broken." I guaranteed her that after a long period of time, her sister would call. I suggested she keep her emotions in check and her thoughts clear of family matters. A year later she called to say that she and her sister had lunch together. They both felt their relationship was now positive for the first time, and conversed together without arguing. Her sister's cancer was much improved. I was pleased she had taken my suggestions and was not surprised with the positive results. Though this story appears psychological, I believe it is related to the way a relationship may impact your health. When you break a cycle based on negativity, health can return to normal.

**JANE:** Victor was being diplomatic in discussing these sisters, and their emotions. To me, the most important aspect of a relationship is not only emotional support but also a willingness to change health patterns. Most people who seek alternative therapies are women. They are more likely to be open to new theories, but very often their husbands, families or friends discourage them. This can stifle women who are hoping to improve their health. Even if you are wearing the right clothing, or have the correct dental work, if negative frequency comes from the people surrounding you, it can prevent a person from moving forward. In a good relationship both people need to be physically and emotionally healthy. Emotional support is very important, but without the physical support it isn't enough.

Since beginning my work with Victor and hearing his thoughts on the importance of healthy materials in all aspects of life, I decided to buy a new couch. Between reading and watching television, I spent a great deal of time sitting on the couch, and even with one of the healthy quilts draped over it, never felt especially comfortable. I asked Victor what he thought, and he agreed that it needed to be changed. Now that I was getting better, anything unhealthy had a greater impact on the way my body felt. My hunt began by going to different furniture stores, sitting on various couches and trying to find real comfort. I knew not to buy anything without Victor testing it first, but didn't want to waste his time dragging him from store to store. I finally found a couch that seemed to suit my quest for health. At our next appointment, Victor went with me to look at the couch. After sitting on it, he thought it was quite good, but did not like the fabric. We looked at different swatches. It was not easy finding one with the right frequency. I wanted something healthy, also attractive since I could not avoid looking at it all the time. Finally we found a fabric we both liked. It was an animal print. We brought the sample to the couch and sat down. Victor draped the piece of fabric over his neck and shoulders. He wanted to be certain it felt right. By placing the fabric over the back of his neck he was able to feel the strength of its influence on the body. The salesmen looked at us quizzically but left us alone. I'm not sure what they thought of Victor as he sat with a shawl of sample fabric draped around his shoulders. I think everyone was surprised when I actually ordered the couch.

**Victor:** I knew the importance of furniture from the time of my arrival in America. My friend had a couch that felt comfortable. I wanted the identical couch for my apartment, the same company, the same material, the same everything. My friend said he would help me buy a better couch. I told him "I don't need better. I want the same." He brought me to a store owned by Russians, and explained what I wanted. After payment, they promised to order me identical furniture. A week later they delivered the couch and love seat. I immediately knew it was not the same as my friends. They told me to try it for a week, and if it still didn't please me, they would take the furniture back. My friend's couch had felt comfortable to lie down on. After lying down on my new couch, my back began to hurt. My muscles felt inflamed. I knew this couch would never let me feel good. If anything, the couch would destroy my health. I called the store to complain, but the owner never returned my calls. I tried to sleep on this couch for a few months. Though continually working on myself, my back muscles ached and I was exhausted. After looking for a time I found an American store that had the same couch as my friend, and ordered it immediately. Within two weeks time the store called saying the couch had been discontinued. About a month later I finally found the right couch. It was available, though not in a color I would have chosen, but I didn't care. It was more important getting a couch that was comfortable and instantly available. With the discovery of how much better it made me feel, came the realization of the importance of the right furniture.

**Victor:** Jane was reversing her condition. She was the first person to do everything I asked of her. She continually proved my theories correct by improving her health condition by following all of my recommendations. I remembered some of the others.

**Memory...** After being in New York for a short period of time, I received a call from a friend living in Boston. Her husband suffered with bad circulation in his legs and was having a difficult time walking. He also was plagued with numerous other health problems. When I saw my friends, the man was leaning on a cane. Nadia approached me and we walked towards the car. Her husband spoke, "You go to the car. I will come later. I can only take a few steps at a time leaning on my cane. I need to stop and rest in between." I wanted to help him, and knew that I could. When we arrived at his house, he told me the doctors wanted to do by-pass surgery on his legs. He had terrible circulation and there was a chance that gangrene would get in his feet. He had already lived through three heart attacks. When he was about to undergo the by-pass surgery prescribed by the doctor, he sat up from the operating table and left the hospital. He knew with his heart condition, he might not survive. The doctor had warned him, "You will never escape from me."

My friend wanted to know if I could help him. "Of course I can help." I remained in Boston and worked on him every day for two weeks. At the beginning, his legs were very thin. His wife Nadia told me how much her husband had changed in the past two years. She watched a strong man become terribly weak. He hardly walked at all, not even around the house. He even hired a special massage therapist to work only on his feet. Socks or regular shoes were no longer possible because they constricted his circulation.

My friend also had an enlarged prostate. His blood work showed a 9.2 level, which was way above normal. The doctor wanted to perform surgery accompanied with radiation. I suggested he hold off for a while to give me time to also work on his prostate. After two weeks I returned to New York. The circulation in his legs had already improved. I began traveling back and forth, each time remaining a few weeks to work on my friend. Gradually the levels in the prostate tests had reduced to 3.2. Below 4 was normal. In a few months time, my friend had fully improved the blood circulation in his legs. He returned to his original doctor for a new round of circulation tests. When the nurse looked at the read out she thought something was wrong. She compared it to his old tests and couldn't believe her eyes. She changed the tape on his legs, and tried again. After repeating this procedure three times, she called for the doctor. This time the doctor repositioned the tapes himself, but the readings always came out the same. The doctor questioned my friend, curious as to how he made such improvement. My friend jokingly answered, "I started drinking four glasses of vodka four times a day. This improved my circulation." The doctor smiled. "Vodka is not going to give you this kind of progress. What kind of drugs are you using?" My friend responded. "I have a friend who is a scientist and a healer. He worked on my legs and my prostate. I am now much better. I used no drugs, no herbs, no vodka. He just touched me with his hands and everything worked." He couldn't explain the why or the how of it, but the results were visually obvious.

**Jane:** Seeing Deborah for bodywork once a week, was part of my routine. I had never stopped since starting with her a few years before. My condition had stayed at the same level for a long time. From the time we began working, my problems were always the same. The range of motion in my arms and my legs was very limited. I was always aching, especially in my shoulders and neck area. My legs weren't much better. Deborah had seen the inflammation bring me to a new low level. She knew how much pain I had been in. It was slow walking the short distance from my car to her studio. It was even difficult getting on and off her massage table. Our weekly sessions continued while I was working with Victor. Deborah was very impressed with the job he was doing. She was able to see how much my condition was changing and looked forward to seeing the new improvements from week to week. She knew all of my limitations in movement and flexibility. She continued to be amazed at the weekly improvements in my condition. I was very happy that Victor felt she had a positive influence on me. She was helping make his job of getting me back to health easier. I was always careful about who worked on my body. I realized how important it was to have only a person who is aware of your entire condition work on you. Deborah had great intuition about what was going on in my body. I had confidence in this intuition and her ability to do the correct things to help me feel better. There was no worry that she could affect me negatively. It made me happy when Victor said he thought she was very good. I knew how Victor felt about many of the various therapy practitioners who were working on people. I had already heard some of Victor's stories about how the wrong person could make your condition worse.

**Victor:** I felt very confident about Deborah's work. She was doing very appropriate treatments for Jane's condition. She didn't cause any damage in Jane's most inflamed areas. Her wrists and her fingers, also her neck and shoulders were the most inflamed. I could feel the shifts she was making in these areas. This was very helpful to me in the beginning of my work. Jane's health frequency was very low at the start. Deborah's work helped me fight the sickness much easier.

**Jane:** By the end of the summer I never felt the rain in advance anymore. It was nice to wake up and find it raining. I was glad to have lost my ability to predict the weather. What a relief. The aches and pains in my shoulders were almost gone. Dr. Horowitz was astounded at the progress I continued to make. Whenever I saw him, he called me "miracle girl." He was amazed that the Scleroderma was actually reversing. I liked to demonstrate all my improvements, first showing him how my hands had changed. There was more strength in my grip. The fingers were opening and closing better then ever. My face looked much healthier. Dr. Horowitz acknowledged I was indeed changing for the better. In his entire career, he had never heard of anyone else reversing the effects of Scleroderma and believed it was a miracle in progress. My condition had reversed more than he would have expected even at that stage. I was positive that with Victor's help my condition would continue to go in a positive direction and achieve a complete reversal. Everything Victor had told me he would do was happening.

Victor was always generous when it came to helping his clients. He heard that the most famous healer from Russia was in the U.S. doing a series of mass healings. The first was to take place in Brooklyn. This was the same healer that produced such a positive response in Victor when he had seen him in Russia. He suggested that all his clients attend the healing event, but being unfamiliar with Brooklyn, I did not want to travel there. Victor then discovered there would be another event in Queens that was closer to Westchester and easier for me to find. He promised to meet me. It was being held in a high school auditorium, which could only accommodate about two hundred people. Victor and the healer knew one another from Russia. The healer spoke only in Russian, so Victor sat next to me to translate. Before the show began the healer approached Victor and began a conversation. He suddenly turned to me and spoke in English. Victor was shocked because he believed the healer only knew Russian. He told me that he wanted to put on big shows. For some unknown reason he believed I could help him with business.

The show began. The healer went to the back of the auditorium and walked slowly down the center aisle approaching the stage. Techno music blasted in the background. He was dressed in black from head to toe, and donned a Julius Caesar haircut. He looked as though he pumped iron daily because his body bulged with muscles. He sat down in a chair on the stage with a table placed in front of him, and spoke in Russian. Victor translated the healer's words but none of what he said made much sense to me. After finishing his talk, people were invited to form a large semi circle on the stage. The healer motioned me to be the last person in the circle. I asked Victor to stand right behind me. I felt much more secure knowing Victor was there to protect me. The healer proceeded to place his hand on a person's head, and within a second the person dropped to the floor. When it was my turn, I spoke to him…"You better not hurt me." He responded in English promising that nothing bad would happen. He touched my head, and I felt a blast of energy run through my body. I saw a column of pure white light that went right through my head with such great force that my knees buckled. The healer held on to my back and lowered me gently to the floor. I lay still for a few minutes while he continued to speak in Russian. Soon everyone stood up and left the stage. My body felt relaxed. It was a strange and unique event.

I thought this healer was interesting, but not nearly as strong as Victor. He might have had healing abilities (Victor certainly felt that he did), but they didn't seem to have an effect on me. Victor's knowledge included all of his theories about how materials affect you. That had made a big difference in my health. Victor's range was much broader, bringing the entire environment into the healing process.

**Victor:** I liked giving Jane examples while we worked, regarding the importance of correct materials. I told her the story of Carol, a woman who had called me through a mutual friend, and eventually became a client. She had recently moved to another state, and our first contact was made by telephone. Carol was a woman in her late fifties who constantly complained about her health. She was always tired, and could not walk much because her feet and legs hurt her. She was plagued with unbearable headaches accompanied by some form of muscle spasms that were terribly painful. There were times she lay in bed for two or three days because it hurt too much to move around. Carol had seen many healers but to no avail; she never felt any better. She tried everything, even moving south for the warmer climate and to swim each day in the ocean. She called me, and asked if I could help her over the telephone, complaining of a bad headache accompanied by muscle pain. I started working on her, and explained the importance of wearing the right clothes made from positive fabrics, also sleeping in the right night clothing. I never expected the reaction I received. She became very emotional and could not believe that anyone other than herself suffered from the feel of certain materials. The sound of her voice was high pitched and excited upon hearing I had found clothes that were both comfortable and healthy. Carol confessed that since childhood she could not tolerate the clothes her parents had bought for her. She tried ripping out the labels. That helped, but the clothes still never felt right. Her parents believed she was mentally disturbed, unable to understand how a child could fuss so much about clothing. They saw her friends wearing similar outfits, and not complaining. They took Carol to a therapist. After their first session together, the psychologist explained to her parents that Carol was not mentally ill, but extremely sensitive to different materials. They had to listen to her choices concerning the clothing she wanted to wear. Whatever the therapist said made no difference, because she could never find clothes to make her comfortable. I explained that her problem with clothing was not only her sensitivity but also the fact that she was powerful. By this I meant she had very strong bone marrow. When people are powerful their body cannot tolerate anything that is not related to the bone marrow's healthy condition. Carol was impressed with my explanation, and asked me to send her clothes by overnight mail. She went on to say she was planning a trip to New York in two weeks time so I suggested that we wait with the clothes until she arrived. Impatience overtook her, and she was in New York three days later. Carol explained she did not want to suffer in her clothes even one day longer. Her desire was to find instant relief, believing she had suffered enough pain already, and was now prepared to feel comfortable. She came to my apartment for a treatment. I told her over the phone that I had put away some clothes for her, and she was anxious to pick them up. I gave her a few t-shirts, and a sweatshirt jacket. She put on one of the shirts and said she felt immediate relief. After her treatment she walked to my closet, opened the door and began rummaging through my clothes. She removed t-shirts, placing them neatly in a pile and told me she was not going to leave my house without these clothes. I never experienced anything like this, and wondered if this was the way some people in America behaved. I became uncomfortable, thinking her parents might have been right about her as a child. Maybe she was slightly crazy. Her strong desire to have my clothes was intimidating. They were my extra healthy clothes, and I was not prepared to share them. It had taken a long time to gather this wardrobe together, as there was little on the market that felt agreeable. It was not possible to replace all that she wanted to take. I thought she might be teasing me, but I was not sure. I put my clothes back in the closet. She took them out again. Carol said she had a little gypsy blood in her, and that was the reason she had no problem shopping in my closet. It was an uncomfortable situation, but also humorous. Because she scared me a little, I gave her a few extra t-shirts. Carol's personality was strange, and though she had ransacked my closet, she did it with a sense of humor. I actually found myself liking her. I certainly never met anyone like her before, and really wanted to help.

At that time there was only one brand of good sheets on the market. I suggested she buy them. Carol became as crazy as me about having enough materials to sustain the right environment. She had suffered all of her life and was overjoyed she could finally find some relief. She immediately bought the sheets.

For the first time someone was listening to me and cooperating, but she had a problem. Each time she came for a treatment she was wearing something wrong. Carol liked to shop and invariably bought unhealthy clothes, clothes with the wrong frequency. I explained that the way she shopped was like throwing money away, because as in the past she never felt comfortable in what she bought. She liked stylish clothes and complained that all the clothes I suggested had no style. I couldn't help it if high styled clothes made from healthy materials did not exist. It was important to remind Carol how she had suffered her entire life from the discomfort of her clothing. Now when she finally found comfort, she complained about style. I continued to tell her to be happy with what she was getting, and believed she was beginning to feel better.

Carol also suffered from a muscle disorder that reminded me of spasms found in people with Cerebral Palsy. It looked similar but I was not sure it was the same. I had never experienced the identical feeling as the one that came from her body. I asked if she ever had a medical exam concerning this condition, wanting to know the test results and the diagnosis of the doctors. She took me by surprise when she admitted never having had a real examination in her life. Carol had spent an entire lifetime trying to discover how to be healthy. She did this all by herself, with little medical support. In retrospect, I think she was afraid of what the doctor's might find wrong with her. She did not want to hear anything negative. To me, this was the wrong approach. It is much easier to deal with an illness if it has a name. I suggested she go through a series of medical tests to receive a proper diagnosis. She refused. There was nothing more for me to do.

**JANE:** This story was interesting to me. I too had tried everything, but always with a conventional doctor's involvement. Until diagnosed with Scleroderma, I was being treated for various conditions. None had been correct. I needed to get a proper diagnosis to know exactly what was wrong with me. Guesswork didn't get me anywhere. It didn't give me the necessary information that would lead to my recovery. I knew after hearing Victor's narration that I had traveled the right path and was now healing.

Everything Victor had promised was becoming a reality, but by the end of the summer he discovered a new problem.

He believed my glasses were impeding my progress. They had metal rims, as did most of the styles at the time. I never thought they might be affecting my condition. Victor explained his reasoning. The healthier the body becomes, the more sensitive it is to materials that are not right. He explained that many people think that when they get healthier, they have more tolerance to materials that aren't right. They think it's like an allergy. When you are cured of what you were allergic to, you are not affected again. With an allergy your body can otherwise be healthy. After getting over it, nothing will trigger a negative reaction. This is totally the opposite from what happens when your body changes from being not healthy to a healthier state. As the body's frequency gets cleaner, healthier and stronger, the contrast of any environmental product that doesn't relate to this healthy frequency starts bothering you more and more. This made sense to me, and when I thought about it, felt something was not quite right with my glasses. Uncertain if the effect was as bad as he said, but because of my trust in his judgment, I decided to get new "Victor approved" eye glasses. He explained that almost all metals have a frequency that is not related to the proper health frequency. The metal eyeglass frames that have a negative frequency will affect the very important area around the eyes and the nose. The bone marrow around the eye area cannot breathe freely because of the frequency of the metal. You have more of a chance of finding a good frequency with plastic frames, although many plastics also have a negative frequency and can affect this area. He continued to speak of his concerns about the many nerve centers surrounding the nose that effect the way all the organs work. When you wear glasses all the time, pressure is placed in this area, and the result is felt throughout the body. The type of glasses you wear can also affect your teeth. The blood circulation in the gum area is small and gentle. Any magnetic field can influence the blood flow. All metals have different frequency fields. It is possible to create electrical fields by attracting these influences from the atmosphere. Not all fields are the same, some stronger, others weaker. Any affect they have on the blood circulation in such an important area is enough to cause damage. Victor's conviction was strong and we made arrangements to meet at an eyeglass store located in the city. Our plans were unexpectedly cancelled.

The next day, September 11th, 2001, changed everything. The entire city closed down. New glasses seemed trivial compared to the catastrophe that hit us so unexpectedly and with so much force. Victor could not think about work because of this unimaginable event. He spoke to no one for a few days. I knew he was reacting to the disaster. Everyone felt devastated. We took a long break, trying to pull ourselves together.

*You can die anytime. Life is so short that you must find a way to be happy. September 11th reinforced my belief that good health was part of happiness. Maybe that was one of the reasons I fought so hard to attain it. Life and death appeared as arbitrary events, random happenings, but working to be well was not arbitrary. I could change my condition. And now more than ever, I believed my journey, and everyone who crossed my path along the way, would only lead to greater happiness. After such tragedy a reevaluation takes place. I wanted to feel more happiness than I ever felt before.*

The city closed down and there was limited access into town, while life started getting back to normal. A few weeks passed before Victor and I began working together again. We continued our search for the correct eyeglass frames. There were a variety of plastic frames to choose from, but Victor did not approve most of them. He held each pair of glasses in his hands for testing. If he thought a pair had possibilities, he tried them on, than walked around the store while wearing the frame. He found one pair that was acceptable. I ordered them, curious to know if I really would feel a difference. Upon receiving the new glasses I wasted no time wearing them. Almost immediately my body behaved differently. A new sensation engulfed me. It felt as if my head was opening, and at the same time the blood circulation in my entire body started moving. It was impressive to feel these differences just by changing eyeglasses. The explanation had made sense, which was why I had changed the frames to begin with. It was always gratifying when a change actually made a big difference.

This spurred me on to find new glasses for my son. After he went to his optometrist and got a new prescription, I knew I had to find something good for him. Brian's eye doctor suggested we visit a local eyeglass store. Most of the frames were made of metal. The plastic frames all seemed to be aimed at girls. There were a lot of nice ones in pretty pinks and purples, but none that were appropriate for a young boy. I described what I wanted, something that looked like the metal ones, but were made of plastic. The owner of the store said they just received a new line that might end my search. They were not children's frames, but Brian and I thought them perfect. Instinctively I knew the glasses felt healthy and ordered a pair for my son. Brian got his new glasses a few days later. When he started wearing them he felt better in general. His allergies seemed to be improving. Before making a purchase for myself, I wanted Victor to see them. He was teaching me to recognize when something was healthy, and I wanted him to see what I had found. Victor came with me to the store. He had never seen glasses like this before. The lenses were of a good frequency plastic. They didn't have a hard, stone like frequency that he often felt from glass lenses. All the connecting pieces were also plastic including the screws that held the pieces together. He found them interesting, and thought they were the best on the market for the health. I immediately ordered a pair for myself and was surprised at the number of people that complimented both Brian and me on our glasses. Victor had his own explanation. He believed the energy frequency coming from the glasses related to good health. This would change the skin and muscle tone of the face, and when people looked at them they felt something. Because they could not explain what it was they were feeling, they just believed the glasses were attractive.

I felt a big difference with these glasses. Even though the last plastic ones I had bought with Victor felt good, these felt even better. They had a lighter feeling about them. They weighed less on my face, but it wasn't only the physical feel to them. I felt much stronger and healthier in general. I was in a better mood because I could feel that my health was continuing to improve. People don't realize what a big affect on your health the wrong glasses could cause. It makes a lot of sense that you could create so much damage. Many people have these metals or other bad materials sitting on their face all day. Your brain is right underneath this area. Victor had told me circulation around the nose is destroyed by this negative frequency coming from the frames. The magnetic fields are also affecting circulation going through the teeth area, to the brain and afterwards to the entire body.

*"Miracle girl," that is what he called me. With each visit, whether every month or every other month, to the doctor, I was always "miracle girl."*

*Reversing my disease was not a miracle. It took a lot of time and effort. Since Victor entered my life I surrendered to complete health. Healthy clothes, sleeping on a healthy mattress, my body relaxing underneath a quilt made from healthy fabric. These simple changes moved me closer to health, closer to happiness.*

*I thought of other times, other scientists who were ignored when they spoke about the dangers of asbestos, lead paint in homes and schools. Everyone said no... these influences could not harm us, nor hurt our children. How wrong they were. Brave scientists continued their research proving the bad effects on our health. People died from these substances. Only then were steps taken to remove toxins from the environment. Now they speak about the horrors of smoke filled lungs, and drinking by pregnant women. Victor is another one of these forward looking scientists putting out warnings. Warnings that materials worn on our body and put in our teeth can profoundly impact one's health. The closer to perfect the environment becomes, the better the chance of all of us becoming "Miracles."*

It was November. I was proud of my achievements, and wanted to share them with the people who helped me along the way. So I went to see Teri Weinstock, the therapist who worked on my hands after the surgeries. She hadn't seen me for over a year, since she had stopped working on me. She looked at me in wonderment, not quite believing the obvious changes. I quickly displayed how much of a fist my hand could make and my good finger movement, but she exclaimed, "Wait with the hands." Teri was looking at my face. She thought I looked completely different. It was now possible to see the elasticity in my skin. She even commented on my frown lines. Whether that was good or bad did not matter. The collagen from the Scleroderma had tightened my skin, almost like a facelift. Now as my skin loosened, lines were reappearing. Teri kept telling me how happy she was for me, and finally looked at my hands. She knew I never exercised myself, but because of Victor's help, enormous changes had occurred. She observed how much closer to a fist my left hand had become, and was so excited she took measurements on the right hand. It showed a large increase in movement. Teri also saw motion in the top joints of my fingers on my right hand. Previously, there was no movement. It felt good to see her truly happy for me. I always liked her. She was terrific at what she did. She was the first person to encourage me to put pen to paper and tell my story.

After leaving Teri's office, I remembered Dr. Horowitz belief that it was quite impossible to reverse my disease. He may have thought I would not be alive to tell my story, given my body's rapid deterioration when I first began seeing him. People can sometimes slow the disease, remain at a level of remission or continue to get worse, but they don't reverse the disease and get better. Scleroderma is not reversible. The effects of this disease can develop over a different amount of time with each person. People react differently. With me the disease started off moving very quickly. I didn't want to keep it at any level I had passed through. They were all less than my goal of complete health. Having faith in being able to reverse this disease, the answer had to be out there. I didn't know exactly how, but I was going to find a way. Victor had the answers I was looking for, searching for. I had suffered long enough, and did not like it. After avidly researching ways to stop the misery associated with my disease, it was finally possible to relax with the knowledge that someday soon life would return to normal. It felt great to be getting my healthy body back.

**Victor:** I felt lucky to be in the U.S. I knew that finding Jane and receiving total co-operation in healing her, rarely, if ever happens. This would help prove my scientific theories about the effect of different materials on the body. No one else had completely followed through with my recommendations before. She could be the proof.

My thoughts turned to the day I went to the American embassy to pick up my visa. My life could have been different had I not received my papers that day. My life, Jane's life, would certainly not be the same, but an incident occurred that allowed me to travel without a problem. Sometimes fate intervenes or maybe just plain luck.

My friend had organized a few conferences about alternative healing methods. They were being held in New York. I was asked to speak. We were standing in line at the embassy waiting to get the visa. Sometimes it was difficult because the embassy always did a thorough background check. A visa was not given to just anyone, and I thought there could be a problem. Being a healer and scientist might not impress the people at the American embassy. We stood on line for almost two hours before even getting close to a window. At that very moment an announcement was made over the loud speaker. A person in the lobby was having heart problems. The embassy had already called emergency, but they needed immediate help from a doctor or nurse. During those years, in the Soviet Union, it could take two or three hours before an ambulance arrived. You could die five times over before help was found. The woman would die unless she received instant attention. It impressed me how differently from the Russians the Americans handled the problem, and had the windows issuing visas closed. All eyes turned to the lady with the heart problem. The staff brought the woman a chair, and helped her sit down. Many people tried to assist the ailing patient. In Russia, you could die waiting on line and no one would even stop working. The line would continue to move right past you. I wanted to help this woman, knowing I had enough knowledge to improve her condition. My friend Alex, held me back. "Don't go over there. You won't get a visa if someone sees what you are doing." This upset me because it was obvious she was close to death. A few doctors standing in line went over to help. They tried to medicate her. She refused the medicine. Her own medicine was in her handbag but she believed there was no hope. I watched as her condition deteriorated, moved towards her, but Alex grabbed me by the coat to stop my advancement. I knew time was running out and removed my coat moving quickly to her side. It was impossible for me to stand by any longer doing nothing. I asked the people surrounding the woman to move back five or six yards and requested they not look at her. The crowd did not leave, insisting they wanted to assist me. I repeated in a loud voice, "Please, leave me. Let me help her. Now!" If anyone had stayed, it would bother me. One woman spoke up, "I am a professor and a heart specialist. I can be helpful if you need anything." This was all a waste of time because I couldn't concentrate if someone was standing close by. I exclaimed, "Please, if you don't want to hear bad words, just move away. You can watch from the side. Don't look directly at us. This could interrupt what I'm doing. When I finish you can come and examine her." Everyone on line respected my wishes. They turned, watching me from the corners of their eyes. I began by working on the woman's shoulders and the heart area, wanting to improve her circulation. She had no energy and almost no blood circulating throughout her body. Her condition was bad, but after working for only two or three minutes, I felt she was beginning to improve. After ten minutes, her breathing changed. The color in her face turned pink. Her circulation got better. She was coming back to life. After another fifteen minutes, a worker from one of the windows spoke to me. He asked if it would be a disturbance if they reopened the windows and began working again. "Of course not," I said. "This woman will be completely normal."

The people at the embassy returned to work as I continued helping her. I saw Alex move up in the line and take his turn. He received his passport and visa, than asked if he could pick up my papers, but the girl at the window refused his request. She said I had to get my own papers. Though my name had already passed, she suggested I come directly to her when I was ready.

I brought the sick woman to a normal condition after working on her about forty five minutes. Her bone marrow had responded very well and was activated. I did not believe she would have any problems for at least two or three years. After finishing my work, I invited the heart specialist to examine her. She took her pulse and listened for her heart beat. The doctor was impressed, and said she heard about healers, but had never seen one at work. It peaked her interest to do research in this direction. I explained my work and we exchanged telephone numbers. She was also going to America for a conference and seminars so we made plans to get together when we returned.

I walked to the window to pick up my passport and visa. The girl thanked me for helping the sick person. Though they had called emergency, the ambulance still had not arrived. While waiting she saw I had brought the woman back to life. She gave me a visa without a problem, and wrote in my passport, "Business conference on biological energy." I was pleased that she understood what I was doing.

**Jane:** Victor told me of this incident at the American embassy. It amazed me that such an event occurred, but I always believed what is meant to be usually becomes known to us. Maybe not immediately, but eventually these happenings are crystallized. By helping the woman at the embassy, Victor was able to attain both passport and visa with ease. This brought him to the U.S. and eventually to me. And now my health is returning. The aches, pains, and operations are slowly fading, but my journey continues.

Taking the Prednisone caused me to gain weight. A combination of the drug, not feeling well, and constantly in a state of exhaustion had me eating more. I gained over fifteen pounds, and was not happy or comfortable with the excess weight. There was an advertisement in the local paper for a weight loss center in my area. I made inquiries by phone wanting to hear their technique. Basically it concerned changing eating habits to only healthy foods, cutting down the intake, and keeping track of everything you ate. It was one on one. A group situation didn't appeal to me, not being interested in other people's struggles with weight loss. I knew I could lose the extra pounds, but needed someone to monitor me. Supplements and protein powders were out. It was just a matter of curtailing my eating. There was a personal trainer working from the same center. She advertised a special price for the holidays. I liked Mardi, and felt positive energy around her. This instilled me with confidence that she would soon have me on a good exercise program. I always needed a knowledgeable trainer tell me what to do while my mind wandered. The combination of exercise and diet worked. It made me feel better. Victor was pleased to see me exercising, and happy I found a trainer who had a positive effect on my body. I believed she was good or I would not have started with her.

**Victor:** Jane told me she had not exercised for a long time because of the pain in her skin, muscles and inflamed joints. Now, after all our work together, there was much less inflammation. Since she had not exercised, she developed some atrophy and lack of movement that went deep into her muscles. The disease process of Scleroderma helps cause a lack of skin and muscle. Even a small amount of exercise to get started is helpful. Now she found a good trainer who could work within her limitations, and not cause problems. Stretching and exercise is always important when the body is not inflamed. Sometimes, small inflammations can be reduced by exercise. The blood circulation can wash out the area that has the inflammation. Through exercise, healthy supplements that are naturally in the body can be brought to the area that is inflamed. After Jane worked with this girl, I tested her response. Immediately, everything started to work in the right direction. There was definite improvement.

When your body starts to warm up as you exercise, your body needs to get the right frequency coming in from your clothing. Since Jane was wearing the correct clothing, it helped to reduce all the stress and muscle inflammation she might have gotten otherwise. This is important for everybody. People who exercise produce a healthy frequency in the process. This healthy frequency is almost always interrupted by the unhealthy frequency of most clothes. Unhealthy clothing creates blockage and minor pain signals. This is especially apparent in professional sports. Very often athletes have muscle injuries. This should not happen to people in good physical condition. When athletes are healthy, they should not need to use steroids or other performance enhancing drugs. Their bodies can work better through natural means. The steroids might help for a short time but ultimately they hurt the body. By being healthy through changing the environment, a person remains fit in every aspect of life. Healthy frequency clothing should not only be worn when exercising or playing sports, but each day, all the time.

Jane began working slowly with her trainer. They started by doing stretching exercises, and weight training. I believed this was helping her become healthier. At first Mardi didn't want to push her too much. This was very helpful. The exercises were not harming Jane's weak muscle areas, and there was no chance of inflammation reoccurring. I had a lot of respect for what Mardi was doing. I continued to activate the bone marrow in Jane's arms, fingers, and body. Her muscles were slowly returning to normal. The exercise helped the muscles work to their full potential. I also suggested some stretching exercises to Jane. These would help in her full recovery from the effects of her disease. These stretches would not be enough without her also working with her trainer.

Though working on Jane regularly, the progress was not going as quickly as I expected. The better your health, the more obvious it is to find existing problems.

One day, feeling I was coming down with the flu, I stopped at the drug store and bought a pain reliever. I showed the tablets to Jane, wanting her opinion. Her response took me by surprise. Jane said she had been taking this product every day for the past two years. She went on to say that she still took two pills every night before going to sleep. Dr. Horowitz had recommended them for pain relief, and believed they would help her sleep. She never considered these tablets as medicine, but I felt completely contrary. To me, it was medicinal. At this stage of her disease Jane still had trouble sleeping. Her muscles continued to ache, and it was hard finding comfort, even with the pain reliever. Whenever I worked on her, I felt something wrong with her stomach. After she mentioned taking these pills, I suspected she might be suffering side effects from taking the medicine for such a long period of time and suggested she stop. It was important for me to know exactly what was happening in her body. This information was necessary for my own work. Jane agreed not to take the tablets. The body has to work naturally. I was aware of something, but she felt nothing. That did not mean it had no affect. When she stopped, there was immediate improvement in her stomach. My work became clearer, and I believed it was the last thing standing in the way for complete recovery. I discovered the medicine also had an effect on other aspects of her health. It had reduced feelings coming from her teeth. These pills are most helpful when used to reverse painful inflammatory diseases, but should be taken sparingly, and only when necessary.

**Jane:** It was interesting to discover the effect of the medicine on my body. I never thought it was important enough to even discuss. Luckily Victor asked about the pills because he knew very little about the different American products. When I stopped taking the medicine, Victor was able to feel a problem with my teeth. He realized he had been wrong in thinking that the materials in my mouth were perfect. Without the medicine masking my true condition, he was able to see that there could be an improvement. Every treatment I had with him had been following the same routine, starting with my left hand, then moving to different areas. Now Victor started working around my mouth also. He placed his had over my face, with the tips of his fingers over the gum area, slightly away from my teeth. After awhile he moved his fingers closer to the teeth. When he worked, I could feel that there was some sort of stress being held in this area. He was definitely right about something being off in my mouth. It was becoming clearer to him that the dental materials were standing in the way of my return to full health. Because he had not yet found perfect dental materials, he only suggested I change a crown on the upper left side of my mouth. This was the one tooth Dr. Gershon had not originally worked on. He had drilled into it, but finding no mercury, he left it alone. I decided to follow Victor's suggestion. He said he had Russian gold coins that carried the right frequency. He gave enough coins to Dr. Gershon to make the crown for me. This gold was unable to hold porcelain on the outside. The crown was toward the back of my mouth. It didn't matter to me if I had a gold tooth back there. No one could see it unless I laughed. Dr. Gershon was not happy to place a gold tooth in my mouth, but he did. Once in place, the gold appeared to change color, and have a pink cast. I liked the color. It was certainly different. Dr. Gershon laughed, and said it was kind of cute.

Victor always encouraged everyone to change their dental work to the right materials. He believed when people do this they become healthier. You also look younger. The skin gets a healthy glow. The face muscles fill out and start to rebuild the structure of the face to a more youthful appearance without the need for plastic surgery. When you are healthier you can remain more active in life. The perfect dental material can save people's health and lives.

### Tanguska, Russia

On June 30th 1908, a giant fireball raced across the night sky. Then it exploded with the force of 1,000 Hiroshima bombs killing herds of reindeer and scorching hundreds of miles of trees. It happened in a remote place in Siberia called Tunguska. The night sky had a strange orange glow as far away as western Europe. The only proof that something happened was a quiver on a seismograph 1,000 miles away in the city of Irkutusk.

Scientists did not come to the sight for another 19 years. When they finally did come, what they saw was a place of utter devastation. They searched for a crater, a piece of asteroid or meteorite but found nothing. They were able to find eyewitnesses in neighboring villages. They recalled that there had been a fireball streaking through the sky, a horrifying noise, and an enormous blast.

From then on there have been many theories as to what happened that early June morning. The theories ranged from meteor impact to an exploding spaceship. Using computer simula-

> TIONS, SCIENTISTS KNOW IT IS A METEORITE FROM AN ASTEROID THAT FRAGMENTED IN THE ATMOSPHERE.
>
> IN 1946, A SOVIET ENGINEER AND ARMY COLONEL WROTE A SHORT STORY EXPLAINING THE DESTRUCTION AT TUNGUSKA COULD ONLY HAVE BEEN FROM A NUCLEAR BOMB, AND THAT SINCE HUMANS DID NOT HAVE THAT CAPABILITY IN 1908, IT MUST HAVE BEEN AN EXPLODING SPACESHIP. THE BOOK BECAME POPULAR IN THE SOVIET UNION AND A GROUP OF SCIENTISTS DECIDED TO FIND OUT IF IT WERE TRUE. THERE WOULD STILL BE MEASURABLE LEVELS OF RADIATION. THEY SEARCHED FOR TWO YEARS BUT FOUND NOTHING.

**Victor:** People are always surprised to know that I work on myself. I reply with a story. It takes me back to Tunguska, a famous place in Siberia. I was working there with a group of men. It was winter and we were driving on ice. We drove along a river close to where the big meteor had fallen in 1908. We had special trucks that could float like a boat if the ice broke. The driver stopped our truck when he saw that that another truck had broken through the ice, and was floating in the water. It was late at night so we were not going to attempt removing the truck from the water. We took the driver and workers out of the truck to return them to the base. We were standing around the truck in the water, deciding how to get it out, when we saw something happening in the sky. It looked like a star coming directly toward us, producing more and more light. We had never heard about UFO's, but this star was coming closer and closer. Though nighttime, the sky became brighter, brighter, almost like daytime. The light stayed overhead for almost fifteen minutes, as if someone was studying us. The crew thought with all this light upon us, we should try to take the submerged truck out of the water. I felt anxious, and believed we should leave, thinking the light might be another meteorite.

And also afraid we could be hit because by now it was directly over us getting closer and closer. I insisted that we leave, sharing my fear with the others. Everyone agreed to return to the truck. As we left, the light moved up, up, and disappeared in the sky. I thought it might be a Russian rocket, but didn't really look like that. The light came directly down, and then reversed course going directly up.

The following day we returned to the truck to remove it from the river. We brought instruments and metal cables to pull it out. The cables had to be placed around the treads that were submerged in the water. The temperature was minus 50 degrees outside so no one wanted to put his arms in the icy water. I volunteered, having no health problems, and feeling strong. I pulled up my sleeves to the shoulder so my clothes would not get wet, then placed my bare arm in the water and put the cable around the treads. It took a long time to complete the job, and my arm felt frozen. The other men warned me I might have a problem in my bones from being submerged in the cold water for so long. I paid no attention, warmed my arm and thought that was the end of it.

The following winter, exactly a year later, my upper arm between the shoulder and elbow began hurting inside my skin. The pain was so bad that I could not sleep. After that I understood how old wounds could haunt people who had lived through war.

My job had me taking long rides. When sitting in the car or in a tractor, I constantly pressed on the bone of my injured arm. Squeezing and holding my left arm with my right hand, believing it might lessen the pain. After a few months of repeating this motion, the pain disappeared. I knew nothing of healing, but without knowledge, instinctively did the right thing. When the problem disappeared, I realized I had healed myself, but did not give it much thought. Everything about this incident felt crazy to me. It was preferable to believe the pain had left on its own. I later learned that almost all the men involved in this incident on the river died from strange accidents. Maybe only one other person, beside myself still lives.

Initially when I started working on people, realizing the problems existing in their bodies made me more aware of what was happening in my own body. If something felt wrong in my body, I worked on myself applying the same method used on my clients. At that time it didn't occur to me I could receive problems from the people I was healing, but after awhile I understood their illness was being incorporated into my body. I had to work on myself to get rid of it and clear myself of the problem immediately. There were times when socializing amongst friends I would get a headache. I tried making it go away by working on myself. Sometimes it got better, but did not entirely disappear. It took awhile before realizing it was not my headache, and searched to find just whose head was bothering me. If I worked on this person my own headache disappeared. This discovery led to the belief that what you feel in your body does not always belong to you. Very often people become ill because they are picking up information through an exchange of frequency of someone else's problem. Their body stores and keeps this information. Modern medicine and tests do not always have answers for people's complaints. There are times the cause is coming from somewhere else.

*I felt myself return to life, a life of routine and normalcy. The capacity to achieve everyday chores freed me. I no longer feared being locked in a bathroom because I could not turn a doorknob. Nor was I forced to ask the doorman to open a jar for me exposing my helplessness over a simple chore. My limitations were now disappearing, becoming a piece of the past. The future looked bright, and I suspected life held many surprises anticipating each one with joy and optimism.*

**JANE:** By February 2002 the range of motion in my arms had improved so much I was able to raise them up easily. For the first time in years there was no problem getting out of my t-shirt by bringing it over my head. Now there was even enough strength and flexibility in my hands and fingers to open a jar or bottle. I was able to hold the cap and actually twist it to open. The seemingly small everyday occurrences that one wouldn't even think twice about were making me very excited. After such a long time of feeling disabled when it came to routine life situations, I was feeling sure that everything was going to completely reverse in my life. My fingers still didn't completely close together, but they were starting to get fuller. I was able to cup my hand with the fingers close enough so water would not flow through the spaces. Now even brushing my teeth could become less of an ordeal. I could use my hand as a cup to hold some water instead of needing a glass of water to rinse my mouth. This was a major improvement. I hadn't really dwelled on my inability to do these little, everyday things that in the past I had always done without a second thought. But it was great feeling like a normal person again.

In April an exciting event occurred. Dr. Horowitz was able to find a vein, and drew blood without a problem. When he saw my arm he exclaimed, "What is that?" "What?" "A vein. Those don't just appear." I had so many veins collapse from the frequent drawing of blood, only never to return. The doctor always had to find a new location, which was never easy. He once again told me I never ceased to amaze him. It was now possible for Dr. Horowitz to use a regular size needle to fill the vials. In the past he could only use a thread needle, and even with such a tiny needle it was difficult. This day in April, I did not even have a black and blue mark. Usually the bruise from the needle lasted for an entire week. This was another indication of how much I was improving from month to month.

I now moved around with no problems, walking up and down the stairs at a normal pace. My routine included a daily walk, and exercising with my trainer once a week. She was surprised by my strength, also impressed as my range of motion showed great improvement. She wasn't the only one impressed with how strong I was becoming. It impressed me even more than her that everything was turning around. Life as I knew it was changing.

Brian was having his Bar Mitzvah at the end of May. This meant it was time for me to once again venture out to the clothing stores. My healthy t-shirts and jeans had to be tucked away for the day, but I would not face the same disastrous results as the last time I dressed up. And certainly was not prepared to lose any more teeth. I felt so much healthier, and did not want to jeopardize my work with Victor. Six weeks before the event, my hunt began for clothes that were both suitable and healthy. Looking through the racks at numerous outfits, none felt right to the touch so they remained on the hanger. Finally I discovered a suit that had real possibilities, rationalizing that if worn over a healthy t-shirt, it would not affect me negatively. I also found a dress that might work, but made sure everything was returnable. Victor would be the first to check the new outfits, showing him I could find relatively healthy clothes for myself. A pair of shoes struck my fancy. They were soft with rubber soles, similar to shoes purchased in the past that had served me well, even when my feet pained from the Scleroderma. I made certain they too could be returned.

It was a relief when Victor applauded my purchases. Now I felt certain no harm would come to me from wearing the new clothes. Truthfully I was overjoyed that I did not have to look further for something else to wear.

The Bar Mitzvah was a great success. The guests enjoyed themselves, and I suffered no discomfort from my clothes. No tooth extractions this time to worry about. I had not seen many friends and relatives for some time, and it was wonderful to find them truly amazed at my improved appearance. The old me finally emerged from all the layers of sickness that intruded and interfered with a good life. The compliments floating my way were appreciated. It had been a long time since I looked healthy. It was a happy day.

I don't remember whom, but someone sang a song "It's been a long time coming." I believed those words applied to me when I looked in the mirror. Now upon seeing my reflection in the glass, the reversal to the old me smiled back. Not being vain, I rarely looked at myself. Having not lost my inner confidence, I had no desire to see the outer changes in my face, or how this disease distorted my features. It was hard enough just seeing my body go wrong. That was enough. I now saw myself as a healthier woman, on the way to recovery.

My improvement continued during the summer months. By October, my hand opened and closed more easily. There was no pain when raising my arms. My wrists were more flexible, my legs moved normally, and upon awakening each morning nothing hurt. The extra tingling in my muscles that signified the Scleroderma disappeared. I could now do everything without giving it a thought. No more aches and pains with each movement. I felt great.

**JANE:** One day while shopping at the supermarket, an acquaintance approached me. She had seen me after the first surgery, when the cast was on my hand, and asked me what had happened. I explained being diagnosed with Scleroderma. Now, she said someone she knew had received the same diagnosis. And because my suffering with this disease had gone on for many years, she wanted to know if I would speak to her friend.

Her friend had two small children and was very depressed, believing her condition was irreversible. I immediately gave the woman my telephone number so her friend could get in touch with me. A few days later she did call, and we spoke for about forty minutes. I was good at giving pep talks, and told her what my condition had been right from the very beginning. I continued, explaining the various steps that had improved my health, placing special emphasis on the dental work. We both suffered with the same disease but I was now better, and spoke from first hand knowledge. I wanted to make her feel stronger, and help to extend her life span. She thanked me for the information and expressed gratitude for giving her hope. She called me back a few days later. She wanted to inform me that she spoke to her doctor, and told him all I had said. He told her not to follow my suggestions, saying I must have a different Scleroderma. There are no different Sclerodermas. There are only different ways to deal with it. The Scleroderma is basically always the same. I later found out, through her friend, that she had died within the year. She listened to her doctor, and believed there was nothing she could do. She thought her only option was death, and so she died.

People who read this can deny it, but they cannot disprove it. All the actions I took made a real difference in my health. And I am here, alive and well to tell my story.

# Víctor: Tapes And Dvd's

I USE THESE TAPES AND DVD'S to raise my own energy level. It also helps to cleanse my body from frequencies I pick up while working on other people. I know if these tapes work well for me, they can help everyone.

Though the tapes may appear to be a form of meditation, they are not. The difference is in the knowledge of the health frequency. People who meditate may find it helpful, but only if they do it alone. I have seen many group meditations where someone is sick, affecting healthy people in the group with low vibration energy. People are sick for different reasons. Those who are powerful can be more affected by the wrong clothes and dental materials. They react stronger than a person with a weaker system, and become an unhealthy frequency. When these people are part of a group meditation, they send out an explosion of unhealthy energy that mixes with the healthy frequencies from the weaker people. This directs the healthy people in an unhealthy direction because of the energetic contact. Those in the group do not realize it. Their bodies record the unhealthy frequencies, and carry it out with them after the meditation. They may become sick. It can work like a virus. When one understands how these frequencies are affected, it becomes easier to understand how these tapes work.

When I make my tapes and DVD'S, I make certain I am completely healthy. It is important to have no dental problems and be dressed in perfect clothing. I discovered a method of recording these healthy frequencies onto the tape. After recording, the finished product is tested thoroughly, making certain it has only a positive effect with no negative frequencies. Knowing the frequencies of different diseases, I can feel what frequency is coming from the tape. If anything is wrong, it can be detected.

These tapes are produced for myself as well as others. My energy tape is different from all the others. I experimented a long time before receiving the desired results. People with various diseases have used my tapes and greatly improved their health. When sick people begin using my tape, the television works like radar. The healthy frequency I recorded goes out from the television or computer screen. The healthy frequency from the screen sends signals into the body, repairing problems people are experiencing. It is not necessary to sit and watch the tape. You can move around the house, because the tapes are healthy for everyone. The signal from the television expands in all directions, reaching into the body, allowing all people in the vicinity to feel and work well.

These tapes are also effective in an emergency situation. If you are sick, the tape can help the body clean out the wrong frequency. If you are taking medication for an illness, the tape will help the medication work to the maximum.

The tapes cannot completely change your condition if you have the wrong dental materials, or other materials of bedding or clothing with bad frequencies. Even so, it will help you stay healthier because it allows the body to feel what is wrong in the surrounding atmosphere. The tape becomes a subliminal teacher. Not everyone is sensitive to the problems in their body. Most people do not know if they are truly healthy. Everything may feel right and routine, so the majority of people do not realize they can do much more for themselves.

The tapes also make my work easier. I gave Jane a tape to help clean her body from the wrong frequency of the disease. When she played the tape while asleep at night, her disease did not have enough time to take control of either her body or immune system during the breaks between treatments. The frequency of the tape reduces skin pain, allowing her body to rest more. The tapes I gave her work on a similar concept to drugs, only without the side effects. After awhile, the disease and the body begin to immunize itself against the frequency of the tape. As with a drug, if you want to receive the maximum effect against a serious disease, you need to change the medication. It is the same with the tapes. After Jane used one tape for a time, she became better. I then gave her another tape from a different time and frequency. It carries the same healthy frequency but because it was recorded at another time, it differs in power and effectiveness. Compare it to a river. A person cannot go into the same water more than once. It may be the same river, but the water always changes. This is the theory behind the tapes. Jane has a full collection of all my tapes. After awhile she discovered by herself, which tape to use for a particular reason. For sleep, if she feels one tape stops helping, she will use another, and continue switching. After not seeing a tape for a long time, you may return to it and experience the same powerful effect on the body.

These tapes direct the health frequency, but without my personal treatments, you cannot always repair the bone marrow to complete health. Even with the tapes, it is important to wear the proper clothing and have the correct dental material. Only then can the tapes reach maximum effectiveness.

# Thoughts

*I SAT ON MY COUCH having a few extra minutes to myself to relax. Though my body felt good, I reached for one of Victor's tapes to add to my sense of well being. It was the first tape he ever gave me, a strong tape for healing. And though I am almost completely healed, I never wanted to fall back, always move forward because my focus had served me well.*

*Thoughts turned back in time. Now that I was feeling well, it no longer bothered me to search my memory, and think of the past. I closed my eyes allowing myself to wander, to muse. I began wearing contact lenses at the age of fourteen, and wore them for almost thirty years. Before any of my strange Scleroderma symptoms fully kicked in, my eyes had started becoming dry. When I put the lenses in they began to hurt immediately. Even the skin around my eyes had become dry and uncomfortable. The eye doctor had given me drops to use before I went to bed at night. My eyes would get so dry while sleeping, the eyelids would stick to my eyes and I couldn't open them when I woke up. By that time, even the thought of wearing lenses made me uncomfortable. My eye doctor told me to stop wearing the lenses or there could be serious damage to my eyes. I recalled with dread the thought of wearing glasses, but had no choice. The lenses had become too painful. I told Victor my story, because the Scleroderma began three years after no longer wearing lenses.*

*I looked at the tape remembering what he said. He thought the signs were clear, believing I had mercury, and other wrong materials in my mouth connecting to the contact lenses. The material from the lenses blocked activity in the bone marrow in my cheeks moving downward to my teeth. Raising my hand to my lips, it was hard to fathom that so many teeth problems derived from the contact lenses. Could all this misery have occurred because I didn't want to wear glasses? At fourteen years of age who wants to wear glasses? In truth it might have spared me, but that is something I will never know.*

*I had worn glasses since I was seven years old, directly after receiving the first fillings in my teeth. Now, all these years later it was clear that those fillings did not have cement compatible to the bone activity in my cheek area, damaging the nerve in my eye and reducing my vision. My entire body was affected by seemingly innocent actions… taking care of eyes and teeth. Victor became even more adamant, saying these fillings may have damaged the brain and nerve activity. Maybe if the wrong materials had not been put in my mouth, none of this would have happened. Maybe? I began to ask people when they first started wearing glasses. Almost everyone gave me the same answer, after receiving dental repairs.*

*I stood up from the couch and stretched my arms above my head. It had become a motion taken without thought. No more pain was attached to it. I was back to being healthy, standing in my living room stretching normally. I thought about changing the tape, but decided against it, instead returning to the couch.*

*A smile crossed my lips recalling the winter I began taking the protein powder recommended at the diet center. Protein drinks were still on my mind. Both now as well as then, I had lost the weight and kept it off. During the summer months it was easy to remain slim with all the delicious fruits available, and weather conducive for taking long walks.*

*From my seat on the couch, Victor's face stared back at me. It had never occurred to me to tell Victor about the protein powder because I considered it a food product, not a medicine or vitamin. He always maintained that food was not as important as the right environment. I was trying to be healthier, wanting to support my lifestyle with proper diet and exercise. The people at the diet center encouraged these products and I finally gave in and tried them.*

*My thoughts became still while I watched the tape, feeling the energy flow into me. The sun made its way into the living room, warming my body that once again reclined on the couch. I tried to pick up my thoughts... Where was I? Protein bars and protein shakes. I remembered how easy it was to have a shake for breakfast or for lunch. In the middle of the day I was always hungry, and ate a protein bar to hold me until dinner. I ignored the fact that myself, or any of my friends, did not especially like the taste, because it kept me from eating. Gradually, the shakes and bars were taking the place of a meal. Smiling I recalled how happy it made me that my weight remained the same. Fifteen pounds, forever gone, never to return.*

*I changed the tape. This new tape produced the same sensations as having Victor work on me. The feelings begin in my lower back and work their way through my body.*

*Returning to the couch I recalled Victor becoming affected by problems in my stomach. He had consistently complained of nausea, thinking it could be a side effect from reversing my disease.*

*I felt the strength and energy of his tape moving throughout my body.*

*I remembered the day Victor called saying his stomach was completely upset, and had no idea where it was coming from. He blamed another client saying she probably started taking protein drinks without telling him. I laughed out loud, smiled at the tape almost as though*

*Victor was present, and seated in the room with me. When Victor had said protein drink I reacted immediately, confessing that I was the one taking it. This shocked him. He was taken by surprise, but finally understood why my stomach felt bad considering all the work he was doing on me. He felt certain he had told me of the ill effect the protein products could have on my health. We had never discussed protein shakes. This was a product that seemed to be only food, nothing that would be harmful. For once, I believed Victor might possibly be wrong in thinking he had told me.*

*A healthy breakfast is one of the most important parts of health. It is an important investment in your daily schedule of energy. When people only have coffee or tea in the morning without any meal, they are pulling energy away from their entire body. Without any breakfast the body has to work very intensely to get enough nutritional supplies for brain and muscle activity. We all get these supplies from our food. If you have no food in the morning, the body starts pulling the nutrition from the muscles, blood and bones. The system has to work much harder to stay at a motion level needed for morning activities. Victor was right when it came to indulging in a healthy breakfast.*

*Once again I laughed out loud in my empty living room. Thinking about breakfast reminded me of a story Victor had told me about McDonalds. I could hear it come back to me in his words.*

*Victor clearly remembered the day the first McDonalds opened in Moscow. It was the biggest McDonalds in the world, and everyone wanted to try the food. People stood on line for more than two hours just to get in the door. Restaurants in Russia held special meaning. They existed only for the rich, but with McDonalds even people without money wanted to go there. It showed status to say you had been to the new McDonalds. It was the only American restaurant in Moscow. Even in the bitter cold of winter, adults with their children waited in line for hours. This place looked different from the other restaurants in Russia. All the workers wore uniforms and were young. Everyone smiled, something that never happened in a Russian restaurant. In many Russian restaurants, if the waitress were angry she would throw the food in your face. You could return home feeling you had been abused. And if you complained about the food they could kick you out. After McDonalds opened, the attitude in other restaurants gradually changed. The Russian workers behavior became different. The cashiers and the people serving the food no longer attacked the customers. Western thought about the customer always being right was beginning to invade the Russian psyche.*

*I found this story humorous. Victor had not thought it humorous when I went for a treatment without eating a proper meal. I agreed to eat a healthy breakfast, though not at McDonalds.*

*The phone rang disturbing my thoughts. I jumped up from the couch and ran to answer it. My son was calling, but only after returning to the living room did I remember the years of hardship in just trying to stand up from a seated position. Now it was easy to get up without thinking and immediately go about my business. I no longer took a healthy life for granted. Every movement brought with it a deep appreciation.*

*I looked at my arms. There was no sign of the psoriasis that had plagued me for twenty- three years. It once covered both my elbows and knees, making them red and scaly. Just to be certain I lifted one leg, then the other, inspecting my knees. Nothing. I sighed with relief, remembering when the Scleroderma arrived the psoriasis disappeared. When I began my work with Victor the psoriasis reappeared.*

*I went back into the living room, returning to my spot on the couch. It had been years, almost a decade to feel healthy and relaxed enough to enjoy a lazy day at home playing Victor's tapes and musing about the past.*

*I recalled Dr. Horowitz' reaction when I happily showed him my psoriasis had returned. To me it was a sign that my skin was returning to normal. He said I might be the only person alive happy to have psoriasis. It had remained at a low level until I began the protein drinks. Then it worsened, spreading down my legs and up my arms. A seemingly healthy product affected every part of me. When Victor told me to stop the protein drinks, the psoriasis was at its worst, and it took a few months before returning to its low level.*

*My fingers wandered through Victor's tapes stacked neatly next to me on the table. I kept them close, in this way making sure they were easily available for my use. I never tired of exploring the different ways my body reacted to a new tape.*

*When the psoriasis attacked me, Victor suggested one of his tapes for skin conditions. My hand touched that particular tape, and I recalled sleeping with it on my TV screen for eight hours each night. After a week my skin cleared. The psoriasis was no longer at a low level. It was gone. Victor's words came back to me. Once again as with all diseases, he believed the psoriasis is connected with healthy bone marrow. I knew his thoughts by heart. "The bone marrow needs to breathe. By wearing the right clothing and having correct dental materials the bone marrow becomes healthier. Everything begins to work properly."*

*Relaxing on my couch and looking at my clear skin, I felt grateful.*

*Lulling about, I lost all sense of time, but suddenly felt hungry. This propelled me into the kitchen. I prepared a large salad consisting of lettuce, tomatoes, avocado and beets. Sitting at the table came the thought that eating had always been one of my greatest pleasures. As I easily brought the food to my mouth it reminded me of days gone by when it was not even possible to grasp a knife. And if I held on without having it fall to the floor, I did not have enough strength to cut anything. Someone else had to cut my food. Even chicken, which is relatively soft, was too difficult for me. At that time my mouth could barely open so everything had to be cut into small pieces. I felt like a child, still too young for a knife and fork. After the dental work was complete, my mouth opened wide enough. My strength returned enough to hold a knife. I did not need the extra help.*

*I was enjoying my lunch while admiring the different shades of green in both the lettuce and avocado, along with the deep purple beets.*

*Cooking gave me as much pleasure as eating. I always loved to cook and was considered quite accomplished. I even attended a cooking school in Italy, specializing in northern Italian dishes. Before my illness I cooked every night, preparing all the food myself. When the Scleroderma arrived it became impossible to handle the various knives needed to chop the carrots, celery, onions, potatoes, and whatever else the recipes required. With my illness I could only do the basics. It was not even possible to lift a pot filled with water to drain the pasta. How could this happen? I had always been a strong woman, but now I couldn't do even the simplest of chores. It became a particularly frustrating experience not being able to use my talents and enjoy a delicious dinner.*

*I finished lunch, placed the dishes in the sink, and wandered back to the living room, once again sitting on the couch. I felt thirsty after eating, and prepared myself a cup of cappuccino. Sipping it slowly because it remained hot, my thoughts turned to sheets. Eating, sleeping, it was all so basic but difficult to get right. Looking at Victor's face looking back at me from the television set made me realize that things I never thought about before, like sheets, now loomed large. I sat back, still holding the cup of coffee in my hand and recalled buying a sheet, and wanting Victor to test it. He felt the sheet, spread it on the couch, then lay on it, placed it over his shoulders, and said it was not perfect but felt quite good. I washed the sheet in warm water with no soap, and put it on my bed.*

*Victor and I then went searching for a perfect mattress. We took my son Brian with us. He was tired and lay down on a mattress displayed on the showroom floor. After testing all the mattresses we walked over to Brian. Victor felt the mattress he was lying on, and then he lay down himself. He found it interesting that Brian had instinctively chosen the best mattress. The mattress was delivered to me a few days later. I put a good quilt on the bottom as a mattress pad. I then placed my new fitted sheet on the mattress. Victor had given me a perfect flat sheet and pillowcase that I had been using for the past year, then a good quilt over the top along with my pillow made from another good quilt. I now believed my bed was nothing short of perfection. Soon I began having pains in my shoulders and back. My psoriasis flared up again on my elbows, returning to where they were before. Scleroderma sensations haunted me. It was unbearable and I could not understand it. Maybe remembering all the misery I endured for so long in trying to get healthy stopped me from addressing the emotions, pain and frustration at the time of my disease. Now in looking back, maybe I was reliving all the aches and pains. I was of two minds because a part of me believed it was something coming from the outside, and did not feel my body was actually succumbing to the Scleroderma again. Victor was also in a quandary, and did not want to worry me. He suggested the possibility that it might be emotions surfacing from memories, but did not really believe that to be the case. There had to be a physical reason from an outside source creating these aches. After three weeks with no let up, Victor checked my bed. We moved it away from the window, because he thought there was possibly something in the wall affecting me. Then he said, "Why don't you try taking the sheet off." He had forgotten that he said the sheet was all right. I removed the new fitted sheet though reminding him that he had said it was fine for me to use. The difference it made with the bottom sheet gone truly amazed me. I enjoyed a good night's sleep and woke up without any aches or pains. All the bad feelings disappeared. I did not call Victor right away, wanting to be certain my body really felt better. Later that day I called him, excited that we had resolved the problem. He was glad to have realized it was only the sheet, but re-enforced his belief that every fabric, even a sheet, made a real difference to my health. My body has become so clear from the negative influence of materials, that I have an immediate reaction if the fabric isn't right. We now realized that "quite good" is not perfect, and will have a negative effect on the health. My progress immediately improved. Though it may be hard to believe that something so minor could make such a big difference, your body will tell you otherwise.*

*Was I still testing? Would I always be testing? I'm sure I will be. As my body gets clearer and healthier, anything made out of the wrong material affects me. Even if I am not aware of it immediately, the feelings soon become apparent. My skin will start to bother me or my joints will start aching. Wearing only clothing that is perfect for my health is the only answer for me to be comfortable. This is not always easy. Many times if we find something perfect, I buy as many of the item as I can. Often, the item will be sold out of the store and not be available again. This happened with the quilts. I'm glad I bought so many, since they no longer are on the market. There are others, but the quality is not as good. I learned to be prepared for the future, trying to cover myself as much as possible by building up a supply of good clothes. It doesn't bother me wearing the same thing everyday. My health and comfort is much more important to me than style. I don't understand how people could feel any differently.*

*My mind raced ahead, thinking about people and their priorities. It seemed strange to me that so many people preferred being sick than try to do something to return to health. Sympathy and attention must motivate them. When some people feel sick, they want you to hold their hand and commiserate. If a person is healthy, he or she is judged by actions and performance without sympathy. To many it must be easier remaining in a sickly condition, be catered to, be waited on, than have to make a life for yourself. It is not an easy path to make the journey towards health. It is easier to do nothing, because for some being sick becomes a way of life. These are the one's that prefer suffering, and not feeling good, believing this is their lot in life.*

*There are people who do not even want to see a doctor, because they fear discovering what might be wrong. I always felt you should see a doctor. If something is wrong, at least you will have a name for the condition and you can deal with it at an early stage. You don't have to continue with traditional western medicine, but at least you have a starting point. You will know what information you will need to deal with the problem. To do nothing seems ridiculous. To not feel good and not see a doctor because you are afraid you might really have a problem does not make sense to me. If you are worried,* DO SOMETHING ABOUT IT. *Not to address a problem does nothing to solve it. Life deals you all different hands, both good and bad. If you choose not to play, you lose out. Life is a continuing adventure. At least be in the game. You might learn something, and enjoy yourself along the way.*

*Spring arrived and the flowers were all in bloom. My flower bed was covered in shades of purple and pink. My two favorite colors. I picked a few peonies to bring inside the house. The flowers really belonged outside springing forth in all their beauty from the dirt and surrounding grass, but one or two peonies on my dining room table would not disturb Mother Nature. And it gave me great pleasure to look upon their beauty. I sat down at the table looking closer at the beauty of the picked flowers. Staring at their shape and color reminded me of a story Victor once told me. I liked calling it The Lady With The Flowers.*

*A woman began working with Victor. She was quite ill, and whenever Victor went to her house, he always found it filled with flowers. He felt concern for her, and in his desire to make her well gave this woman a healthy quilt, also shirts made from healthy material. After a period of time, the client's health improved, but her house remained filled with flowers. She told Victor her many friends sent them because they cared so deeply for her. (And believing she was at death's door displayed their feelings by sending flowers.) Victor had sighed and told her soon the flowers would stop because she was becoming so much healthier. The woman objected saying her friends would always send flowers. Her health steadily improved. The test results were encouraging, and the flowers stopped coming. About two weeks later the woman called Victor, claiming she had added up his costs for the following year, and decided not to spend the money anymore. Victor was frustrated but felt there was no point in arguing. If she wanted to keep her money and remain at the same health level, that was that.*

*Her body eventually was unable to sustain itself without his help, and she died. I'm sure that once again her house was filled with flowers.*

*I sat up, stretched my arms and was happy I was a person who wanted to know, desired the truth if something was wrong. And then go about changing it.*

*When I began seeing Victor, it was obvious to me that he had power, but working with Victor takes time, no instant fix. I had been deteriorating for six years before meeting him, and never expected an instant cure. A lifetime of environmental influence takes time for the body to clear if you do everything perfectly.*

*Victor and I were on a parallel course. I had already finished my dental work before meeting him, and always dressed casually wearing comfortable clothes. Even being headed in the right direction, it still took years to completely heal. My resolve was to find the answer, and though not knowing where or who, I never gave up looking. It was not in the stars for me to die from a disease. My determination to be healthy never wavered. The only alternative was to die. I was lucky to have found Victor, but also happy that I was able to realize that he did have the answers for me. By following his direction, which led me back to health, I knew his theories were correct. The difference in my body and my life was obvious. I couldn't understand the people he had worked with before who chose fashion or holding on to their money as more important than health. We all make our own choices in life. My choice was to do anything I could to return to health.*

*I remained still for a moment, and knew the time was passing. A day to myself was rare, and I thought about how to spend the rest of the afternoon. The sun was shining, but the weather felt cool, a perfect time to take a walk. Once outside, walking alone near a wooded area,*

*I recalled the time I had cried out in frustration on a morning walk in Central Park. Those days were over, gone forever. Now I looked back dispassionately. My eyes traveled upward at the sky, and knew the Universe had sent me a message. Life would never again be as I once had lived it. After my hands were hit, not being able to work at my artistic endeavors meant losing my creative soul. Making jewelry for twenty years was a large part of my life, and how I identified myself. After the Scleroderma, it took years for me to come to terms with the loss of my hands, creating incredible pain to even look at jewelry. Visiting the gallery that had once displayed my work became very frustrating. It only re-enforced what I had lost, and a large part of who I used to be, leaving me no idea which direction to go in to find what I might become. Only now, looking at jewelry does not give me the sense of loss that had once overcome me. My life has changed direction. I have accepted and embraced that. My outlook has to only move forward, not dwell on the past.*

*It was a beautiful day, and still having a lot of energy, continued walking. My eyes noticed the many cracks along the path. I never allowed myself to crack. From the beginning of my illness, any feelings that surfaced were instantly channeled into determination. My one focus was to reverse the disease. Any feelings other than optimism were blocked from my mind. And it was not just for me alone. I had a child to keep healthy, happy and secure. I knew many people who took drugs to relieve their anxieties. That does not work for me.*

*The dogs marched past me, along with their owners dutifully taking them out for a walk. It made me happy watching them. Even though not the best part of my life, my illness had been a part of living. If it will not kill you, it makes you stronger. I continued walking, knowing all my pain had been left behind. I felt grounded in my own reality of making the called impossible, possible. I reversed my disease.*

*My pace quickened feeling light of foot, happy, and physically stronger than ever before. Even at the peak of health, I never felt as strong. While seeing my house in the distance, I knew I could deal with most anything. Life no longer could throw me any curves. Upon opening my front door, I knew my search would continue. Now the quest was to remain healthy, happy, and have the power to share my knowledge.*

# Final Thoughts and Attitude

WORKING ON THIS BOOK, BROUGHT back all the memories about my feelings while going through my journey. It made me angry, thinking about all the people who I had dealt with who were less than honest in their dealings with me. I became furious all over again at the chelation doctor and the doctor who gave me the live cell treatments. The way they tried to take advantage of my situation upset me very much. While they were doing it to me, then obviously, they were doing the same to all of their patients. I started reliving all the pain and frustration I had gone through at the time. While it was happening, I couldn't let myself give in to all these feelings. I had to keep going forward by myself until I found the answers.

I get angry with people who profess to heal you but in truth are only out to increase their pocketbook. They are taking advantage of people who are sick and often desperate, but are not aware enough to follow their own intuition when it comes to their body. These people believe the hype these practitioners create around themselves and pay them the inflated fees for useless information. My search always continued until I found someone who actually made me feel better in any aspect of my healing process. There were many people who truly tried to help but were just not informed enough about the true cause of most health problems. These people deserve credit for trying to do their best.

The doctors and practitioners who helped me the most were the ones that were the most accessible right from the start. Every doctor that I ultimately continued working with, had a long conversation with me, often before an appointment was even scheduled. They always returned my calls if I left a message, and were always willing to discuss any concerns or problems that might have come up. I made sure to receive copies of all lab tests from every doctor. It was always easier at a first appointment with a new practitioner, if I brought all of my test results from previous lab work.

I am supremely fortunate to have found the right doctors and other practitioners. I am especially lucky to have found Victor. It took time and research to find the right people to help me. The many recommendations by friends and family certainly helped. I always looked into the therapies that seemed to make sense to me. There were quite a few attempts which produced no results, but all seemed worth a try. To just consult one doctor and take a bunch of pills without looking any further, never made any sense to me. I feel that one has to try everything possible to get healthy. There are so many different opinions as far as which direction to take, it's worth trying a variety of different solutions. If I had listened to the original articles read at the beginning of my journey towards health, it is possible my condition would be getting progressively worse. I might even be dead by now. Instead, I am close to complete health and have successfully reversed a previously irreversible disease. The final answer came with the awareness that by using correct materials in every aspect of my life, I was able to reverse the Scleroderma. This change in your environmental influence will affect not only autoimmune diseases, but all conditions no matter how small or major the disease.

I hope that people will read this, and realize that they have to take their health into their own hands. There are many people out there who can reverse their bad health. They can become healthy and stay healthy. I had to change my life to do that but it was worth it.

If a person feels they are being misdiagnosed or are given no clear answers to their questions, they should feel free to look into alternative resources or even contact other doctors who might supply the correct information. Maybe some doctors will be angry about being told they are misdiagnosing your disease. It doesn't mean they are bad doctors, but with so many different symptoms appearing it is difficult to come up with a name if the doctor is not familiar with that particular disease. It is especially difficult with the various autoimmune diseases, because many can have similar symptoms. People have to realize that they have to continue looking until they find the correct diagnosis, and ultimately the answers in order to reverse their condition.

I want everyone to know they too can have control over their lives and health. Every person has different symptoms and manifestations of disease. The thing that remains the same is your response to these conditions. You have to keep a positive attitude and determination to overcome whatever is thrown your way. It is important to do a lot of research into your condition and speak to as many different people as you can. Attitude becomes the most important part of dealing with life. If you think positively, and that nothing can stop you, you can achieve whatever you set out to accomplish. A return to complete health was my goal. I didn't let anything stand in my way. And here I am – Alive and Healthy. It takes forbearance, courage and luck, but I am living proof that it is possible.

This wasn't written as a how-to book. I didn't even particularly want to write a book, but discovering how specific materials in your environment create all sorts of health problems pushed me to write this and share the information I uncovered. It is very important for everyone's health.

Scleroderma is one of the most deadly of the autoimmune diseases. My reversal of Systemic Scleroderma through a change of the materials surrounding me, from dental to clothing to bedding and furniture, should bring hope that not only Scleroderma, but all of the autoimmune diseases may prove easy to reverse.

I hope this book makes your journey shorter than mine.

# A Comment from Dr. Horowitz

JANE PARKER'S REMARKABLE STORY OF her battle with Scleroderma is a testimony to one person's will and determination to overcome a disabling and potentially fatal connective tissue disorder.

Jane's Scleroderma manifested with years of progressive skin tightening despite treatment with Penicillamine, a medication used to promote skin softening. Because of severe hand skin tightening, Jane suffered digital contractures and open infections. Eventually she required corrective hand surgery. She had a severe inflammatory episode at the onset of her Scleroderma requiring treatment with Prednisone in high doses. She had a similar inflammatory episode after four years on Penicillamine, which necessitated the discontinuation of this medication. Jane sought the recommendations of many alternative healers during the course of her illness, most of which were of no help. She did have a short term regression of her skin tightening following removal and replacement of her amalgam dental fillings.

When Jane began working intensively with Victor Dyment her condition took a dramatic turn for the better. She was able to taper off Prednisone within six months. Over the past three years in which she has worked with Victor her Scleroderma has reversed completely. She remains without any digital ulcerations or infections. She is on no medication at the present time and remains in a complete clinical remission.

Mark D. Horowitz M.D., P.C.

For more information on Victor's theories
please visit his website
http://www.healthfrequency.com

ISBN 1-41206291-8
9781412062916